PROCLAIM
SALVATION

PROCLAIM SALVATION

Preaching the Church Year

David Ewert

HERALD PRESS
Scottdale, Pennsylvania
Waterloo, Ontario

Canadian Cataloging-in-Publication Data
Ewert, David, 1922-
    Proclaim salvation : preaching the church year
    ISBN 0-8361-3608-X
1. Festival-day sermons. 2. Salvation - Sermons.
3. Sermons, Canadian (England). I. Title.
BV4254.3.E94 1992   252'.6   C92-094712-3

The paper used in this publication is recycled and meets the minimum
requirements of American National Standard for Information Sciences
—Permanence of Paper for Printed Library Materials, ANSI Z39.48-
1984.

Bible quotations are used by permission, all rights reserved, and except
as indicated are from the NRSV, *New Revised Standard Version Bible,*
copyright 1989, by the Division of Christian Education of the National
Council of the Churches of Christ in the USA; cf. DE, David Ewert;
GNB, *Good News Bible;* KJV, *King James Version;* NIV, *The Holy Bible, New
International Version;* REB, *Revised English Bible;* RSV, *Revised Standard
Version;* TLB, *The Living Bible.*

To the late J. A. Toews,
for many years president
of the Mennonite Brethren Bible College—
teacher, friend, and colleague in the Gospel ministry—
who by his example modeled expository preaching

Contents

Preface

Week after week every minister of the gospel must ask the question: What shall I preach next Sunday? This is particularly true in the so-called free churches, which are less bound to a liturgical calendar. However, it would be a pity if we disregarded the Christian calendar altogether. It helps us to recapitulate the history of God's great redemptive acts.

Christianity is a historical faith; it is not simply a system of thought. It rests on the unique and unrepeatable events by which the kingdom of God broke into human history in the person of Jesus Christ. These saving acts of God in Christ are the foundation on which the Christian church is built, and the church would be greatly impoverished if believers did not constantly remind themselves of their spiritual roots.

As members of the new people of God, we have good precedent for observing the historical events in which our faith is anchored. Old Testament Israelites had three pilgrim festivals during which they relived those events which made them God's people. These festivals (Passover, Pentecost, and Tabernacles) served to keep the memory of God's saving acts alive.

We understand, of course, that the fundamental truths of the gospel can and should be proclaimed in every time of the year. However, the Christian festivals provide natural settings for rehearsing those unique events in the life of

Christ which open up for us the wells of salvation.

The great Scottish preacher James Stewart writes, "The great landmarks of the Christian year—Advent, Christmas, Lent, Good Friday, Easter, White Sunday, Trinity—set us our course, and suggest our basic themes. They compel us to keep close to the fundamental doctrines of faith. They summon us back from the bypaths where we might be prone to linger, to the great highway of redemption. They ensure that in our preaching we shall constantly be returning to those mighty acts of God which the Church exists to declare." [1]

The Christian year begins not with the first of January, but with Advent, and that is where this volume of sermons begins. Busy pastors will find in them some helpful materials which they may use on those special occasions which seem to come round only too quickly. However, I also hope that laypeople will find the following chapters edifying and inspiring.

All the sermons published in this volume have been preached in churches here and there in Canada and in other countries. This means that the language is popular and that an effort was made to avoid theological jargon. For the most part they appear here exactly in the form in which they were preached.

The sermons in this collection are all expository. A biblical text is analyzed, outlined, and then expounded and applied to the life of twentieth-century believers. Topical sermons may be easier to prepare, but they tend toward shallowness. It takes time and energy to wrestle with a biblical passage—with its setting, its language, and the nuances of its vocabulary—and then to draw out some of its implications for the life of the church today. However, there is always something exhilarating about such expositions. They contribute greatly to the growth of hearers in their Christian faith.

Now I invite the reader to walk with me through the Christian year and to reflect with me on the great verities of the gospel.

—David Ewert

1. Advent

The Mystery of the Incarnation

Since, therefore, the children share flesh and blood, he himself likewise shared the same things, so that through death he might destroy the one who has the power of death, that is, the devil, and free those who all their lives were held in slavery by the fear of death. For it is clear that he did not come to help angels, but the descendants of Abraham. Therefore he had to become like his brothers and sisters in every respect, so that he might be a merciful and faithful high priest in the service of God, to make a sacrifice of atonement for the sins of the people. Because he himself was tested by what he suffered, he is able to help those who are being tested. (Heb. 2:14-18)

We have entered the Advent season. Together with Christian believers all over the world, we want to re-live once again the great moment in history when our Lord took on flesh and became one of us.

The early church did not celebrate Advent. In the first few centuries, the followers of Jesus were focusing so much on the lordship of Christ, that they paid less attention to his birth. They did not even remember the date of his birth. Easter was celebrated regularly, and by the second century Pentecost was observed, but not Christmas.

As the Christian faith spread all over the known world of the Roman Empire and open hostilities against the church diminished under Constantine, Christians began to celebrate not only Christ's birthday, but also the weeks of Advent leading up to this day. Advent even came to be seen as the beginning of the church's year.

From time to time there were strong protests against the church's Advent and Christmas celebrations. Some Protestants thought they smacked of Romanism. Moreover, it was pointed out that the Gospels put much more weight on the death of Jesus than on his birth. Early colonists in Massachusetts were even subject to a fine if they made Christmas a holiday. The Christian church, however, has been greatly enriched by its Advent celebrations. So in spirit we join with our many brothers and sisters around the world as we remember once again our Lord's incarnation.

Advent is the first gleam of Christmas. It heralds the invasion of this planet by God's representative, his ambassador, Christ, God's Son. For almost two thousand years in creeds, hymns, and sermons, the church has confessed that in the fullness of time "the Word became flesh and lived among us" (John 1:14). The word *incarnation* means to take on flesh.

Some theologians were not content with confessing this great truth. They also wanted to explain the incarnation in one way or another. Some thought Christ's body was not real; he had only the appearance of a man. Others wondered whether he had two wills, a divine and a human, or just one. And so it went. Indeed, the incarnation is a mystery that takes us out of our depth. It is a mystery not only in the sense that we cannot explain its nature. It also boggles our mind to think that God in his infinite mercy should be willing to visit our rebellious race, and that Christ should become a link in the long chain of sinful human beings. "O love beyond all telling, that led thee to embrace, In love, all love excelling, our lost and human race," sings Paul Gerhardt.

The writer to the Hebrews has something to tell us about this mystery of the incarnation. We begin by seeking the reason for the incarnation.

The Reason for the Incarnation

Since, therefore, the children share flesh and blood, he himself likewise shared the same things (Heb. 2:14). In the eleventh century lived a monk by the name of Anselm. He was a learned man and wrote a number of theological treatises. Among them is a book entitled: *Cur Deus Homo?* (Why Did God Become a Human?). The answer to that question is given, in part at least, in our text: because we are flesh and blood.

Flesh and blood describe our humanity in its weakness and mortality. When Jesus said to Peter, "Flesh and blood has not revealed this to you" (Matt. 16:17), he meant, no human being ever told you that. Paul reminds us that "flesh and blood cannot inherit the kingdom of God" (1 Cor. 15:50). As human beings, with bodies subject to the ravages of sickness, old age, and death, we are not fit to enter the eternal state. For that we need a different kind of body, not one of flesh and blood.

But because we are flesh and blood, Christ shared in our humanity and partook of the same nature we have. He entered the human race the way we do: through a human mother. To be sure, he was conceived by the Holy Spirit, but his birth was like that of other babes. Our Lord was without sin (Heb. 4:15), but he was fully human. And by becoming one of us, he is able to bring us back to God.

It makes little difference from which perspective we

look at Jesus. He always appears delightfully human. Physically he looked like other Jews. Although the Gospel writers are not interested in the color of his eyes or the length of his hair, they portray him as a flesh-and-blood character. He ate and drank as other people did. He got hungry, tired, and thirsty. He had brothers and sisters. He had an occupation. And when the soldier drove his spear into his side, blood and water came out.

From the emotional side, too, Jesus is refreshingly human. He loved people; he had friends; he expressed indignation at the hardness of peoples' hearts. He felt sorrow; he wept; he had compassion. He experienced disappointment and gladness.

Jesus' humanity is seen also in his relationship to God. He was a man of prayer. He confessed he could do nothing of himself, but that he was entirely dependent on his Father. He prayed with "loud cries and tears," we are told (Heb. 5:7). He died with a Jewish child's bedtime prayer on his lips: "Father, into your hands I commend my spirit" (Luke 23:46). To live in dependence on God is to be truly human. We were created so to live.

But Jesus was without sin. Adam and Eve were fully human before they fell into sin. Sinfulness is not what makes a person human. To be without sin does not mean, however, that Christ does not understand sin or that he cannot empathize with the sinner. C. S. Lewis writes in *Mere Christianity,* that "to know drunkenness you have to be sane; to study sleep you have to be awake; to know sin (really know it) you have to be good." [1]

Why, then, did Christ come into the flesh? Because we are flesh and blood. Having given a reason for the incarnation, the writer of Hebrews goes on to speak of the purpose of the incarnation.

The Purpose of the Incarnation

To Destroy the Works of the Devil

So that through death he might destroy the one who has the power of death, that is, the devil (Heb. 2:14). In Scriptures the devil stands at the head of all evil powers that have plagued the human race throughout its long history. This sinister personage is bent on one thing only, to destroy God's creation and to lead humankind into eternal ruin. Ultimately he is the cause of all the pain and woe that people have to endure in this life. Death and darkness, deceit and despair, sickness and sorrow—these all can be traced back to the great deceiver of humankind, who is, as Jesus put it, "a murderer from the beginning" (John 8:44).

Our modern sophisticated Western society finds it hard to fit the Bible's teaching about the devil into its worldview. The irony of it is that just when secular people thought we were rid of the silly notion of a devil, we had an invasion of the occult, black magic, astrology, and Satan worship. We had better not pretend to be wiser than our Lord, who took this enemy of God seriously. From the temptation in the wilderness into the darkness of Gethsemane, Satan pursued our Lord relentlessly. He knew that Christ's coming spelled the end of his reign over the lives of men and women.

Christ spoke of the strong man who keeps people in his power. Jesus, the Stronger One, by becoming a human being, enters the house of Satan, binds this strong man and robs him of his prey (Mark 3:27//Luke 8:22). "The Son of God was revealed . . . to destroy the works of the devil," writes John in his first letter (1 John 3:8).

In the words of Hebrews 2:14, Christ has made the devil "inoperative" by his incarnation. The verb (Greek: *katērgeō*) means to put out of commission, out of work, out of operation; to render ineffective. Jesus came to "destroy" the devil *(Good News Bible),* has to "crush" the devil *(Mof-*

fatt), "to take away all the power of the devil" *(The Jerusalem Bible)*. By the coming of Jesus, the devil's rule was shattered; his dominion was shaken to its very foundations.

One striking proof of the defeat of the devil in Jesus' lifetime was his casting out of demons. "If it is by the finger of God that I cast out the demons," said Jesus, "then the kingdom of God has come to you" (Luke 11:20//Matt. 12:28). By a word of command Jesus expelled demons, and that was a sign that Satan's empire was crumbling. And when the disciples returned from their mission and reported that the demons were subject to them, Jesus said, "I watched Satan fall from heaven" (Luke 10:18). Christ's coming assures us of Satan's demise.

As our Lord stood in the shadow of the cross, he announced the end of Satan's rule. "Now is the judgment of this world; now the ruler of this world will be driven out" (John 12:31). When our Lord hung on the cross in utter weakness and shame, the devil must have grinned with satisfaction. But in that very moment he received his mortal blow. By our Lord's death and resurrection, he snatched the scepter from Satan's hands.

To be sure, for the present time death continues to do its devastating work. But beyond death is life, eternal life with God. Yes, Satan is still at work, and because he knows that he has little time, he musters all the evil forces that he can gather against God and his people. But in the end he will be cast into "the lake of fire and sulfur" (Rev. 20:10).

The last sermon Dietrich Bonhoeffer preached in prison was on the blessed hope of the believer. Immediately after the sermon he was led away to his death. On his way out he said to a fellow prisoner: "This is the end; but for me the beginning of life." And with that we have introduced the second purpose of the incarnation as stated in our text from Hebrews.

Deliverance from the Fear of Death

And free those who all their lives were held in slavery by the fear of death (Heb. 2:15). The first sad consequence of Adam and Eve's disobedience was that they were afraid. From that day on until now, the fear of death has hung like a thundercloud over the human race, threatening to overwhelm us. Fear of death is a powerful taskmaster. Because of fear of death people will do things that would never occur to them otherwise.

Our text assures us that Christ by coming to us has broken the bondage of the fear of death. When John was banished to the Island of Patmos, he had an overwhelming experience one Sunday morning. In a vision he saw the risen Christ stand before his eyes, and he fell down before the Lord. Christ then gently laid his right hand on John and said, "Do not be afraid. . . . I was dead, and see, I am alive forever and ever; and I have the keys of Death and of Hades" (Rev. 1:17-18).

Hades, the abode of the dead, this vast domain, is now under Christ's control. Those who belong to Christ do not need any longer to be in bondage of the fear of death. Paul ends his great resurrection chapter with a triumphant outburst: " 'Death has been swallowed up in victory.' Where, O death, is your victory? Where, O death, is your sting?" (1 Cor. 15:54-55).

Jesus' life also ended in death. In fact, the shadow of death fell on his path almost from the time he was born. Moreover, he died a terrible death, a death on the cross. But his death was not final. Death did not have the last word to say. Christ took on our human nature and carried it through death into an endless life with God, and now Christ asks us to follow him.

On that first Christian Easter, Christ looked into the grim visage of the monster, Death, and slew him and freed us from his grip.

> Love caused thy incarnation;
>   Love brought thee down to me.
> Thy thirst for my salvation
>   Procured my liberty.
>
> *(Paul Gerhardt)* [2]

Christ came to "free those who all their lives were held in slavery by the fear of death." That's the purpose of the incarnation.

The Scope of the Incarnation

For it is clear that he did not come to help angels, but the descendants of Abraham (Heb. 2:16). When we speak of the scope of the incarnation, we are asking, how far did Christ reach when he became human? Our text seems to restrict the benefits of the incarnation to the descendants of Abraham, but let us not be too hasty in making that judgment.

Clearly, the incarnation is not aimed at the salvation of angels. Christ took on human nature; he did not become an angel to redeem angels. But what does the writer mean when he says that Christ was concerned with the descendants of Abraham?

The language of our text comes from Isaiah 41:8-9, where it is said that God took Israel to himself. Israel, the descendants of Abraham, was chosen by God to be a blessing to the whole world. Through Abraham all the families of earth were to be blessed (Gen. 12:3). This blessing of Abraham has come to all people through Christ. Christian believers are now called "children" or "descendants of Abraham" (Gal. 3:7). In our passage, then, all the people of God, both of the old covenant and the new, are included.

However, someone might respond: But did not Christ come to save the whole world? the entire human race? "For God so loved the world that he gave his only Son" (John 3:16). Yes indeed, but only those who believe in him enjoy the benefits of his incarnation. And all those who believe are descendants of Abraham, for they have the faith of Abraham.

So, then, Christ did not become an angel in order to save angels; he became human in order to save the human race. He did not descend from heaven to the level of the angelic world; he came down much lower. He stooped down to his earth and identified himself with a lost and fallen race. He took hold of us, says our text, just as God took hold of Israel and delivered his people from Egyptian bondage (cf. Heb. 8:9).

Jesus was born in a specific place here on earth, and not a very respectable one at that. He became a member of a specific race: "salvation is from the Jews" (John 4:22). He belonged to one of the tribes of Israel, the tribe of Judah (Matt. 1). He was the eldest son of a family and had brothers and sisters (Mark 3:32).

Later, when unbelieving Jews became the fierce enemies of the church, some Christians found it hard to accept that Jesus came from Israel, and that salvation is from the Jews. Some copyists later changed the word of Jesus to the Samaritan woman, "Salvation is from the Jews," to "Salvation is from a Jew." In that way at least, one could divorce Christianity from the Jewish race as a whole. And that was long before scholars during Hitler's regime attempted to get rid of the Bible's Jewishness. Jesus was born in order to save the "descendants of Abraham"—both the old and the new people of God.

The story is told of a first-century Jewish rabbi whose son was killed by the Romans. He witnessed more atrocities when the Romans crucified Jewish Zealots, among them some of the young men of his own village. Later he was heard praying in the synagogue: "God of Abraham, Isaac, and Jacob, you created our body, but you have never had your blood poured out. You have no body to ache and to die. You haven't experienced human grief. You ask us to love you. How can we love you? How can we believe in your love for us if you do not share our human suffering?" If only he had known and believed that God did exactly that when Christ became human and laid hold of us in order to bring us back to God!

The Blessings of the Incarnation

The blessings of the incarnation are too numerous to mention at this time, but our text singles out two. The first of these is described for us in verse 17: *Therefore he had to become like his brothers and sisters in every respect, so that he might be a merciful and faithful high priest in the service of God, to make a sacrifice of atonement for the sins of the people* (Heb. 2:17).

Our Merciful High Priest

The writer here uses Old Testament cultic language to describe Christ's work of redemption. Our Lord is portrayed as a high priest who makes atonement for the sins of the people. We remember that on the annual day of atonement, the high priest carried out the prescribed ritual for the removal of sins for the people of Israel.

In order to serve as mediator between God and Israel, the high priest had to be an Israelite himself. To have a non-Jewish high priest would have been unthinkable. In the United States only a person born in that country can run for president. Landed immigrants, legal aliens, may not run, even if they have lived most of their lives in America. Our text underscores the fact that Jesus had to be made like his brothers in every respect. He had to be fully human, so that he might be a merciful and trustworthy high priest who can serve as mediator between God and us.

In some respects Jesus stands in contrast to Jewish high

priests, who were expected to restrain their feelings of pity. Philo wrote of the ideal Jewish high priest: "He will keep his feeling of pity under control." But our high priest is full of pity. Also, he is trustworthy. That's more than could be said of any number of Jewish high priests who strove for political power. Often they worked hand in glove with the Roman authorities; they were involved in clever political machinations and really did not seek the good of their own people. Some even accepted bribes. But our high priest is completely trustworthy and faithful.

In the Heidelberg Cathechism the question is asked: "What benefit do you receive from the holy conception and birth of Christ?" Answer: "That he is our Mediator. And that with his innocence and holiness he covers in the sight of God [the] sin in which I was conceived and born."

To have a high priest who genuinely cares about us is an uplifting assurance. People all around us (and we ourselves) are in trouble: "I have lost a loved one," says one. "I have suffered severe financial loss," moans another. "I have just received bad news from the doctor," cries a third. Where shall we turn? Is there anyone who understands? who can help? Yes indeed, there is. We have a merciful high priest. Jesus Christ became one of us. He knows what it means to go through life with all its trials and tragedies.

A person physically fit finds it hard to understand someone who easily tires and is often sick. A student who is clever and learns easily finds it hard to appreciate those who learn slowly and who have to plod. A person who has never sorrowed can't really understand the pain of someone in grief. But we have a high priest who cares and can come to our side, as the final verse of our passage suggests.

Christ Is Able to Help Those Who Are Tempted.
This is the second blessing of the incarnation, mentioned by our author. *Because he himself was tested by what he*

suffered, he is able to help those who are being tested (Heb. 2:18).

When our Lord was here on earth, he endured not only the trials of life common to human beings, but unusually subtle and sharp temptations by the devil. Satan did everything within his power to prevent our Lord from going the way of obedience to the Father, the way of the cross. And after the devil had tried every possible angle in tempting our Lord, the devil left "for a season," "until an opportune time" (Luke 4:13). He waited for the next appropriate moment when he would attack again. In fact, one of the most severe temptations seems to have come through the leading apostle, Peter, who wanted to keep Jesus from going the way of suffering. Our Lord conquered by rebuking Peter, "Get behind me, Satan!" (Mark 8:32-33).

And when our Lord entered upon the agony of Gethsemane, Satan attacked him once again with all the fury of hell. But in obedience to the Father, our Lord faced the shame and the suffering of the cross and came forth triumphant over Satan and all evil powers. And because of his triumph over temptations, he is able now to help those who are being tempted. That includes you and me. The word *help* (Greek: *boētheō*) is rather picturesque. It means to run when someone cries. As a mother or father may run to the aid of a screaming child, so our Lord hurries to our side when we are tempted.

All of us have temptations. We may not all have the same temptations; the temptations of a fifteen-year-old are not the same as those of a sixty-year-old. The temptations of parents may be different from those of children; those of the teacher different from those of the students; those of the employer different from those of the employee. Yet there are temptations that are common to all of us: to act selfishly, to be arrogant, to be self-sufficient, to live for pleasure, power, and fame—to mention but a few. But because our Lord was tempted and came through his trials victoriously, he can come to our aid.

There may be some who are quite overcome by the attacks of the evil one. Our text makes it crystal clear that Christ conquered this enemy of our souls. There may be others who are in the evening of life, and the thought of death hangs heavily over them from time to time. Our text assures us that Christ can free us from the bondage of the fear of death. There may be someone who feels totally forsaken. Take courage! You have a merciful high priest whose heart goes out to you and who will come to your aid when you call. Some may feel overcome by temptation, defeated, and ashamed. "Because Christ was tempted, he is able to run at the cry of those being tempted." With that assurance, let us move through this Advent season—and the years that God may be pleased to give us.

2. Christmas

Good News of Great Joy

In that region there were shepherds living in the fields, keeping watch over their flock by night. Then an angel of the Lord stood before them, and the glory of the Lord shone around them, and they were terrified. But the angel said to them, "Do not be afraid; for see—I am bringing you good news of great joy for all the people: to you is born this day in the city of David a Savior, who is the Messiah, the Lord. This will be a sign for you: you will find a child wrapped in bands of cloth and lying in a manger." And suddenly there was with the angel a multitude of the heavenly host, praising God and saying,

> *"Glory to God in the highest heaven,*
> *and on earth peace among those whom he favors!"*

(Luke 2:8-14)

A little boy stood before the picture of his father, who had been away from home for a long time. He missed his dad sorely, and as he gazed at his picture, he said wistfully, "I wish father would step out of the picture." That's precisely what happened at Bethlehem. When the time was fulfilled, God sent his Son in the likeness of human flesh. God stepped out of the picture in the person of Jesus, our Lord and Savior.

That's good news; that's the gospel of Advent. And that

was the message of the heavenly messenger to shepherds in the fields: "I am bringing you good news of great joy."

The Greek word for *gospel* (*euangelion*) means *good news*. In secular society it meant any piece of good news. It also had technical meanings: Caesar's speeches, his decrees, were also called good news (*euangelia*). A decree, dated 9 B.C., marks the birthday of Augustus and reads like this: "And whereas the birthday of the god [Augustus] was the beginning for the world of good news (*euangelion*) that has come to me through him . . . Paulus Fabius Maximus . . . has devised a way of honoring Augustus."

We all know that the birthday of Augustus did not usher in the millennium on earth. However, quite unknown to Augustus, whose decree brought Joseph and Mary to Bethlehem, the birthday of Jesus ushered in a new age, an age of joy.

There was little in the circumstances of his birth that suggested the beginning of an age of joy. Moreover, there was much sadness and gloom in the world into which Jesus came. But the people who sat in darkness were now to have light (cf. Matt. 4:16; Isa. 9:2). Our passage informs us that when God's hour had come, the darkness of midnight was lit up by the glory of God and the heavenly messenger shouts the overwhelming words into the blackness of human history: "I am bringing you good news of great joy."

And that's the announcement we need to hear today as we remember Christ's birth. To us it may be old news, but it's good news, and by the Spirit of God working in our hearts, it can become good news once again. Let us ask ourselves, first, who the original recipients of this good news were.

The Humble Recipients of the Good News

In that region there were shepherds living in the fields, keeping watch over their flock by night (Luke 2:8). Those of you who have been to Israel no doubt have visited the Shepherds' Fields, about two miles from Bethlehem. No one really knows the exact spot where they tended their flocks on that unforgettable night. But in those same fields where David used to tend the flocks of his father, humble shepherds heard the good news.

I say *humble* shepherds, for they were a despised lot in Jesus' day, in spite of Israel's long pastoral tradition. They were accused of failing to keep the ceremonial laws. They pastured sheep in dry areas, where water for washings and ritual ablutions was not readily available. They were suspected of thievery. A popular idiom had it that shepherds did not know the difference between *mine* and *thine.* They were not allowed to give testimony in court. Devout Jews were instructed not to buy wool, milk, or meat from shepherds. In fact, a Jewish commentary on the Shepherd Psalm has this pejorative statement: "No position in the world is as despised as that of the shepherd" (Ps. 23).

The shepherds in our passage may well have been devout men who with others waited for the consolation of Israel (Luke 2:25). The angelic visitations in the Gospel stories are regularly to godly people. Be that as it may, the good news of great joy was announced first of all to lowly shepherds.

That shepherds should be the first to hear the good news of Christ's birth is quite in keeping with the coming of Jesus as a whole. He wasn't born in Caesar's palace. He came from an insignificant village, Nazareth, not even mentioned in the Old Testament. He was born in Bethlehem, "one of the little clans of Judah," as Micah puts it (Mic. 5:2). Jesus was born, not in a modern hospital, not even in a home—the custom at that time—but in a barn or a caravansary. Several early church fathers mention Jesus' birth in a cave. Barns were sometimes made by digging into the side of a hill, so their suggestion is plausible.

Jesus was born of an insignificant peasant girl from Galilee. "Can anything good come out of Nazareth?" asked Nathanael (John 1:46). And when Mary sang her Magnificat, she made special note of the fact that God had scattered the proud in the imagination of their hearts and had put down the mighty from their thrones (Luke 1:51-52). When our Lord defined his mission to his synagogue hearers in Nazareth, he said:

> The Spirit of the Lord is upon me,
>   because he has anointed me
>   to bring good news to the poor.
> He has sent me to proclaim release to the captives
>   and recovery of sight to the blind,
>   to let the oppressed go free,
> to proclaim the year of the Lord's favor.
> *(Luke 4:18-19)*

Notice that the recipients of the good news are all disadvantaged people—poor, captives, blind, enslaved.

The good news of great joy came to humble recipients in the first century of the Christian era. It still does. The kingdom of God belongs to those who are poor in spirit. Others have no ears for this message—those who are self-sufficient, who live out of their own resources, who want to live independently of God and his grace. Yet the message of Advent is good news indeed—for those who are only too keenly aware of their needs, who are often overcome by weaknesses, who look for rays of hope in the midst of darkness, and whose hearts cry out for help to God.

From the recipients of the good news of great joy, let us now turn to the bearer of the good news when it was first proclaimed.

The Divine Messenger of Good News

Then an angel of the Lord stood before them, and the glory of the Lord shone around them, and they were terrified (Luke 2:9). A single angel appears at first. Later a vast multitude of heavenly messengers joins in the announcement of the good news of Christ's birth.

All the great events surrounding Christ's coming are attended by angelic messengers. Here they announce the birth of the Christ child. After our Lord's conflict with the devil in the wilderness, the angels are there, ready to serve him with food (Matt. 4:11). An angel strengthens him in Gethsemane (Luke 22:43). Angels are on the spot when Christ is raised from the dead (Matt. 28; Mark 16; Luke 24). When he ascends into heaven, they appear to the perplexed disciples. And when in God's own time this age comes to an end, Christ again will appear in glory with his holy angels making up his entourage (2 Thess. 1:7).

The angel that proclaims good news to the shepherds is quickly enveloped by the glory of God. The Greek word *doxa*, glory, did not have that meaning to begin with. But then the Jewish translators of the Old Testament used *doxa* to render the Hebrew word *kabod*. Thus they filled *doxa* with new meaning and depth, for *kabod* signifies power and dignity, majesty, brightness, and splendor. The word came to be associated particularly with the manifestation of God. For the glory of the Lord to shine around the shepherds meant that God was making himself known. Little wonder that they were afraid!

Long ago God's servant Moses dared to ask God, "Show me your glory," and he was told that no one could see God and live. God then promised Moses that he would hide him in the cleft of the rock and cover him with his hand, and then he would let his glory pass by, so that Moses could at least get a glimpse of God from behind (Exod. 33:18-23). God lives in an unapproachable light (1 Tim.

6:16). When Isaiah, the prophet, saw the glory of God in the temple he cried out, "Woe is me! I am lost!" (Isa. 6:5). It should, then, not surprise us that these shepherds are overwhelmed by this manifestation of the glory of God.

This display of the glory of God is to be the source of joy and gladness. In the person of Jesus, God's glory is to be seen in new ways. John writes, "The Word became flesh and lived among us, and we have seen his glory . . . full of grace and truth" (John 1:14). Indeed, John speaks of the cross as the manifestation of the glory of God (John 17:1). There the fathomless love and grace of God appears in a splendor never seen before.

The good news of a great joy is proclaimed to the shepherds by a heavenly messenger who can be trusted and relied upon. It is unfortunate that newsmen do not have the reputation of being entirely believable in our day. Malcolm Muggeridge tells of the time he spent in Moscow as correspondent for the *Manchester Guardian*. The Soviet censors would not permit factual reports to be sent to Western papers, so he used to make up news to send to his paper.

But here is news that can be trusted. It comes from God; it is mediated by his messenger, a heavenly agent. This is good news; it can be believed, received, enjoyed. Indeed, one can stake one's life on it! But we ask, what makes the message of the angel good news?

The Profound Significance of the Good News

A Message That Calms Our Fears

But the angel said to them, "Do not be afraid" (Luke 2:10). In October 1981, some 200 doctors, nurses, psychologists, and social workers met in San Francisco for the third annual phobia conference. Under discussion were the many kinds of fear that plague people in our society: the fears of people, of being buried alive, of flying, and so forth—even the fear of having peanut butter stick to the roof of a person's mouth. Interestingly, the most common fear these days, according to the president of the society, is technophobia, the fear of technology. People are afraid of the devastating potential that lies in the various fields of technical research in our day.

The French existentialist, Albert Camus, called this century "the century of fear." The message of Advent is: *Don't be afraid.* That's the message of the angel for those of us who are afraid of failure—a common fear that haunts so many people. It is a message of assurance to those whose hearts are full of fear of want. People lose their jobs; unemployment insurance runs out; sickness in the family drains the financial resources available. Where are we to get the money for housing and clothes and daily bread? These are the kinds of fear that grip millions of people in the third world, but we are not exempt from these concerns either.

Who doesn't upon occasion fear that sickness or tragedy may strike down one's own self? Many of our seniors fear old age with all the debilities and limitations and weaknesses it tends to bring. Children and young people also have fears. Recently I was informed that there is a book circulating which tells young people how to commit suicide without undue pain. How sad! Some are afraid to live, others are afraid to die. And then there is that awful fear that humankind may destroy itself by its own folly.

Here is the good news of Advent: *Don't be afraid.* God sent his Son to die for us, and this is a God whom we can trust. God created us; God redeemed us; God sustains us; and when our last hour comes, God will take us home to glory.

Who will separate us from the love of Christ? Will hardship, or distress, or persecution, or famine, or nakedness, or peril, or sword? . . . No! [No! No!] . . .

For I am convinced that neither death, nor life, nor angels, nor rulers, nor things present, nor things to come, nor powers, nor height, nor depth, nor anything else in all creation, will be able to separate us from the love of God in Christ Jesus our Lord.

(Rom. 8:35-39)

The good news of Advent is that we need not be afraid. But there is more in the angel's message.

A Message of Salvation

To you is born this day in the city of David a Savior, who is the Messiah, the Lord (Luke 2:11). One of the great titles given to our Lord is that of *Savior*. That in fact is the meaning of the name Jesus. "You are to name him Jesus, for he will save his people from their sins" (Matt. 1:21).

Jesus is an adaptation of the Hebrew *Joshua*, or *Jehoshua*, and means *Yahweh saves*. It was not an uncommon name among Jewish families. Familiarity with the name no doubt has led to a neglect of its root meaning. (When we say good-bye, no one thinks of its origin in the wish, "God be with you.") Yet when this name Jesus was given to the Christ child, the name Joshua (Jesus) received a much more profound meaning—he saves from sins, he delivers from evil, he rescues us from the enemies of our souls.

The word *savior* was common enough in the ancient world. The gods were sometimes called saviors. People addressed Poseidon as savior, and above all Zeus, the chief of the gods, and also Asclepius, the god of healing, the savior of the sick, the diseased.

Statesmen and rulers were often called saviors as well. The word became particularly popular in the Caesar cult. As early as A.D. 68, Galba, who succeeded Nero, had coins minted with the words around his head, "The salvation of the human race" *(salus generis humani)*. Such human saviors might deliver a country from economic depression, they might save a nation from invasion, but they could not deliver from the chains that enslave all people: the bondage of sin and guilt and fear and death.

To you a savior is born, says the angel, meaning this birth is for your benefit, your advantage, your salvation. "It is clear that he did not come to help angels," says the writer to the Hebrews (2:16). With whom then is he concerned? With us. The child's birth, adds the angel, will bring *great joy for all the people.*

Some copyists later felt that even such an all-embracing proclamation could be understood too narrowly. Some readers might think that *all the people* means the Jewish race. Thus Tatian, the Syrian who in the second century made a harmony of the Gospels called the Diatessaron, changed *all the people,* to "the whole world," so that there should be no misunderstanding. Every man, woman, and child is to hear the message of great joy!

The good news of Advent is that there is deliverance now from the bondage of sin and guilt. This note has been captured by hymn writers who have enriched the life of the church with their Advent songs.

> Come thou long expected Jesus,
>   Born to set they people free....   *(Charles Wesley)*

> O come, O come Emmanuel,
>   And ransom captive Israel....
>   *(Anonymous 12th-century Latin hymn)*

> I lay in fetters groaning,
>   Thou cam'st to set me free....
>
>   *(Paul Gerhardt)*

Today is the day of salvation, for unto us is born a Savior, who is Christ the Lord.

There may be those who have not yet experienced this

salvation, this deliverance which Christ offers. There may be some who have wanted for some time to come to the Savior but didn't quite know how to go about it. I remember when as a youth I wished someone would speak to me and show me how I could receive the Savior into my life! Speak to your parents; speak to the pastor; ask some friend in whom you trust. The good news is too precious to neglect. Hence, the writer to the Hebrews asks, "How can we escape if we neglect so great a salvation?" (Heb. 2:3).

The Heavenly Confirmation of the Good News

The Confirmatory Sign
This will be a sign for you: you will find a child wrapped in bands of cloth and lying in a manger (Luke 2:12). This largely resembles some Old Testament stories in which God establishes his Word by giving a confirmatory sign. For example, when God called Moses to deliver Israel from Egyptian bondage, he gave him a sign to confirm what he had said.

Here the sign is a babe in a manger. What a paradox! A moment ago the angel announced the birth of the Savior, the Christ, the Lord, and now he says you will find a baby, in swaddling cloths, in a manger. To be tightly wrapped in strips of cloth was not at all unusual. It was the regular way of wrapping a newly born babe in those days and was thought necessary to keep the limbs straight. A child wrapped in this way would be easily recognized by the shepherds as a newborn.

What is exceedingly unusual, however, is that the child would be found lying in a manger. It shows the great poverty of our Lord, who although he was rich, yet for our sakes became poor, so that we through his poverty might become rich (2 Cor. 8:9). The reason for laying the child in the manger has already been given by Luke earlier in the story. There was no place in the inn—at least not for an expectant mother. There is no reference to ox and ass in the biblical account. Hundreds of years later they were sneaked in, probably on the basis of Isaiah 1:3, where the prophet complains, "The ox knows its owner, and the donkey its master's crib; but Israel does not know."

The birth of Christ in such adverse circumstances has often been a source of encouragement to those overwhelmed by the adversities of life. Dietrich Bonhoeffer wrote from his prison at Christmas 1943: "I dare say Christmas will have more meaning and will be observed with greater sincerity here in this prison than in places where all that survives of the feast is its name. That misery, suffering, poverty, loneliness, helplessness, and guilt look very different to the eyes of God from what they do to man; that God should come down to the very place which men usually abhor; that Christ was born in a stable because there was not room for him in the inn—these are the things which prisoners understand better than anyone else."

The Confirmatory Message

And suddenly there was with the angel a multitude of the heavenly host, praising God and saying,
  "Glory to God in the highest heaven,
    and on earth peace among those whom he favors!"

(Luke 2:13-14)

When God's hour strikes, then things happen *suddenly.* Malachi had promised that the Lord would "suddenly come to his temple" (Mal. 3:1). When the first Christian Pentecost had arrived, "suddenly" there was a sound of a rushing wind (Acts 2:2). Paul said that when he was on his way to Damascus to persecute Christians, "about noon a great light from heaven suddenly shone about me" (Acts 22:6). Nothing stops God when his time has come. Suddenly a great company of the heavenly host join the angelic messenger and shout doxologies.

When a child was born in Israel, local musicians would often congregate at the house and greet the new arrival with music and song. But no one came to the manger in Bethlehem, and so these minstrels of the heavenly world perform what earthly musicians failed to do on this occasion. They sing, *Glory (doxa) to God in the highest.*

We explained earlier that *glory* means *the majestic, brilliant presence of God* (see Luke 2:9). Here, however, glory is the response to the manifestation of God's glory. In this use, the word means *praise*, as in our word *doxology*. When the angels or human beings give God glory, they praise him for his wondrous deeds. And since God is thought of as dwelling in the highest place in the heavens, the angels give glory to God *in the highest heaven*, the dwelling place of God.

The other part of the couplet brings us down to earth: *On earth peace among those whom he favors!* Peace in the Hebraic sense of the word includes salvation, health, well-being, wholeness, and fullness of life. It is not simply the cessation of strife or war. The Hebrew *shalom*, which stands behind the Greek word for peace (*eirēnē*), sums up all the blessings of salvation. And these blessings are now available on earth, where the human race lives. They come from heaven, certainly, but they are offered to those in whom God is pleased, upon whom his favor rests, and that includes all of humankind.

The older English versions read *good will to men*, but that is a translation based on inferior manuscripts. The message of the angels is salvation, wholeness, peace for those upon whom God's good will rests, his favor, his pleasure. Literally, the Greek reads, *Peace on earth among humans of his pleasure,* meaning people whom God is pleased to save. It says nothing of showing good will to other people; that is something *we* are commanded to do. Instead, this praise speaks of the delight, the pleasure which God takes in bringing salvation to this sin-cursed earth. God's peace and salvation come to earth, to all people, because God loves them.

This is the message of grace. God, in his infinite goodness and mercy, has decided to save the human race from eternal ruin, and he sends his Son to rescue humankind from sin and death and damnation. Instead of visiting us with his wrath, he comes in the person of his Son and offers us *shalom.*

With that kind of message from the heavenly world, the shepherds cannot sit around much longer. They take off immediately for Bethlehem to see for themselves what God had done and to assure themselves that the message of the angels was not simply a figment of their lively imagination. And when they arrive, they find that it is exactly as they were told, and they return, glorifying and praising God for all they have heard and seen. They hear the good news of great joy, and they can't keep it to themselves.

In England in the eighteenth century, the bishop of London warned his parishioners against the "new gospel" that was being preached by the evangelist George Whitefield. Whitefield replied that he was in fact preaching a very old gospel, the gospel of salvation by grace. It only sounded new to many of his hearers.

We have listened once more to the message of Advent. Now some of us may be inclined to say, Well, what else is new? I know that story backward and forward.

Perhaps we have proclaimed it too poorly. Sometimes when one interprets these marvelous gospel stories, one feels as if clumsy hands are touching something of exquisite beauty. But when we stand before God, we will not be able to say, We never heard the gospel. If you will allow God's Spirit to invade your heart, your life, you will discover that this "old" gospel can become new and fresh. And for those who have embraced the gospel with the arms of faith, let us make sure that during this Christmas season we spread the *good news of great joy*.

3. Year's End

My Times Are in Your Hand

Come now, you who say, "Today or tomorrow we will go to such and such a town and spend a year there, doing business and making money." Yet you do not even know what tomorrow will bring. What is your life? For you are a mist that appears for a little while and then vanishes. Instead you ought to say, "If the Lord wishes, we will live and do this or that." As it is, you boast in your arrogance; all such boasting is evil. (James 4:13-16)

We have come to the end of another year. It's December 31 on our calendars. Calendars are practical human inventions. For our method of counting months and years, we are indebted to Julius Caesar and to Pope Gregory, who made some corrections in the Julian calendar in the sixteenth century. God, however, does not measure time in that way. A thousand years in his sight are like a day (2 Pet. 3:8).

The constant change of the seasons of the year may lead us to think of time as cyclical, as though history constantly repeats itself. We take tomorrow for granted, as a mark on time's wheel that keeps forever turning. But in the Bible, the years don't circle. Time moves from eternity to eternity. And somewhere on that long continuum of time, we are granted a few brief years. They are given to us not by some mechanical law, not by right, not because we deserve them, but only by the covenantal mercies of God.

And so at the end of the year, we pause for a moment to think on the grace and the patience of God by which we were allowed to complete another year. These are three hundred and sixty-five days received from the hand of our heavenly Father.

The psalmist David long ago came to the conviction that the days of his life were beyond his control, and he expressed this in a great confession: "My times are in your hand" (Ps. 31:15). This confession is a suitable title for the passage of Scripture we have just read.

The apostle James addresses a group of people in our text who had not yet come to this conviction. They were all too clever about making plans for the future. With his vigorous prophetic style, James pulls them up short.

In the churches to which James addressed his letter, there were merchants, traders, and mariners. Paul's first convert in Europe, Lydia, was a businesswoman. The business persons addressed in our text are forward looking. They plan carefully, their datebooks are full of entries, they leave nothing to chance.

But somehow we feel there's something wrong here; there's something missing. And we don't have to wait long before James tells us what it is. These people behave as if they were the masters of their fate, the captains of their souls, the lords of their time, the managers of their life.[1]

We do not know whether James had Christian Jews in mind. However, as new cities sprang up in the wake of the conquests of Alexander the Great, Jews were often the first to move there. In Roman times, Jews were sometimes lured to the cities by the offer of citizenship; wherever they went, trading was brisk. In any case the letter is to Christians, for who else would read this letter?

James comes down a bit hard on those entrepreneurs, and that makes some of us feel better, since we don't belong to the business class. But we can't get off the hook that easily. James is not bashing businesspeople because they have chosen that calling in life. He criticizes them for their arrogance: they think they have life under control. Yet that's a temptation we all face. Thus our text encourages us to learn the lesson which the psalmist was beginning to learn, when he confessed, "My times are in your hand." Let us then turn to our text and listen to what it has to say to us! We begin by observing that it is possible to deny this humble confession of the psalmist.

Denying This Humble Confession

Come now, you who say, "Today or tomorrow we will go to such and such a town and spend a year there, doing business and making money" (James 4:13).

By a False Sense of Security

There is no suggestion here that these entrepreneurs were going to use underhanded methods to make gain, or that they intended to drive hard bargains. James is not even condemning them for wanting to make profit. One cannot indefinitely carry on a trade or business without profit. Paul says that "whoever plows should plow in hope and whoever threshes should thresh in hope of a share in the crop" (1 Cor. 9:10). Without profit a business goes bankrupt.

What James is concerned about is the false security, the presumption of these adventurers. He is not attacking businesspeople for doing business; he is not criticizing people for having a good business sense. But these men were looking for security in their own ability, in their own astuteness, their own wise planning.

This has been the besetting sin of Adam's race ever

since the fall into sin in the garden of Eden: to live autonomously, to live out of one's own resources. "You will be like God," said the serpent, "if you will eat of the fruit of the forbidden tree" (based on Gen. 3:5). To be like God means to be self-sufficient. God doesn't need anyone or anything. God doesn't need to ask for anything. God is totally autonomous. God created human beings with the intention that they should live in dependence on God. But in our fallen state, that's precisely what we don't want. And this desire for independence from God and his grace has created a world of trouble for us.

James warns against this sin of living independently of God, this temptation to have complete control of our own lives, this false sense of security. And the Word of God, which is alive and sharper than any two-edged sword, comes to you and me today and warns us against looking for security in ourselves as we face a new year (Heb. 4:12).

Perhaps we enjoy good health, we have acquired certain skills, we may even have a good education. We have a considerable amount of native ability, as we say, and some may even have a good bank account, a good pension, or other resources. For all these gifts, we want to thank God. But let us remember that they can all be taken away from us at any time. The youth is snatched away by an accident; the middle-aged person is discovered to have incurable cancer; a hardworking laborer suddenly loses a job; and earthly treasures can vanish overnight. Therefore, we want to confess that our security lies in God and not in ourselves.

There is another way in which we can deny the psalmist's humble confession: "My times are in your hand." It is by making our plans without acknowledging our dependence upon God.

By Making Plans Independently of God

One gets the impression that these businesspeople were assembled around a map. They decide: you go there, I'll go here. With considerable flourish, they announce that either today or tomorrow they will depart for trade and for profit. The time of departure, the destination, the one-year length of stay, and even the outcome of "making money"—these all are determined.

We should not infer from James's criticism that it is wrong to make plans. It would be a pity if we entered the new year without any hopes or aspirations, confident that we will muddle through in one way or another. Nor do we speak the language of faith when we say pessimistically, O why make plans; this world is shortly coming to an end anyway? Instead, as long as it is day, we have a task to perform, a calling to fulfill, a mission in this world. And it is perfectly legitimate, even necessary, that we make plans. However, we must not make them independently of God.

If we confess, "My times are in your hand," then we make plans. When these plans go awry, we take our disappointments out of God's hand; if they succeed, we give him the glory.

And so we want to pray to God that we might not deny this humble confession, "My times are in your hand." As we turn once again to our passage in James, we notice that the apostle goes on to underscore the importance of making this confession, and the reason we ought always be willing to make it (James 4:14).

Recognizing This Profound Truth

Our Human Limitations

Yet you do not even know what tomorrow will bring (James 4:14). One could also translate: ". . . since you are such who know nothing of tomorrow." We are people with serious human limitations. That's an observation that has been made by sages both ancient and modern. But today it comes to us as a Word of God, reminding us that because of our limited knowledge, we should put our life into God's hands. We do not know the morrow.

The worldling, who also realizes that only the present is his, may respond by saying: Right: and for that reason I am going to live for today. Thus *carpe diem* (pluck/seize/grasp the day) was an old Roman slogan. "Eat, drink, and be merry, for tomorrow we die," is the motto of millions of earthlings (cf. Eccles. 8:15; Luke 12:19; 1 Cor. 15:32). But such a hedonistic philosophy has a hollow ring to it. The matching lifestyle leads ultimately to frustration and boredom and the gnawing feeling of meaninglessness.

"You know nothing of tomorrow." We are not the architects of our destiny. We are not the lords of time, of circumstances. The psalmist says,

As for mortals, their days are like grass;
   they flourish like a flower of the field;
for the wind passes over it, and it is gone,
   and its place knows it no more.   *(Ps. 103:15-16)*

The wisdom from above teaches us, "Do not boast about tomorrow, for you do not know what a day may bring" (Prov. 27:1).

There is yet another reason we should consider seriously the profound truth of confession, "My times are in his hand": our life is so ephemeral in nature.

The Ephemeral Nature of Life
What is your life? For you are a mist that appears for a little while and then vanishes (James 4:14). James goes on to ask: "What is your life?" He gives his answer: "You are a mist" or *atmis,* the Greek word from which *atmosphere* is derived. It can mean *vapor* or *smoke* or *mist*—perhaps the mist of the

Mediterranean hills, so familiar to seafaring merchants. The *Good News Bible* compares our life to a "puff of smoke, which appears for a moment and then disappears" (James 4:14b).

Now James is not encouraging us to develop a morbid occupation of our minds with imminent death or possible disaster. The Baptist preacher of London, C. H. Spurgeon, tells of monks in a monastery who greeted each other every morning with the salutation, "Brother, we must die." Spurgeon thought a more cheerful greeting should be recommended. However, if we want to have a realistic view of life we have to take death into account.

When I was a student at Prairie Bible Institute, the president, Maxwell, divulged that he thought of death every day, and he wasn't nearly as miserable as we seemed to be. He had come to terms with the transitory character of our life, while we preferred not to think about the limits of earthly life. C. S. Lewis in his *Letters to an American Lady* points out that there are only three possible attitudes toward death: To fear it, to desire it, or to ignore it. The last of these, he suggests, is the worst, and yet it is the most common of all.

The English scholar Bede, who lived in the seventh century, records that when King Edwin of Northumbria was confronted with the Christian faith, his chief counselor gave him the following advice: "The present life of a man, O king, seems to me, in comparison [with] that time which is unknown to us, like to the swift flight of a sparrow through the room wherein you sit at supper in winter . . . the sparrow, I say, flying in at one door, and immediately out at another. . . . So this life of a man appears for a short space, but of what went before, or what is to follow, we are utterly ignorant. If, therefore, this new doctrine contains something more certain, it seems justly to deserve to be followed."

The realization that our lives are ephemeral adds depth to living here on earth. We have sniffed the air of eternity, and that adds the dimension of eternity to our daily routine.

"Then, at our best let each be living, Full soon will sound life's evening bell. Be this our aim to find our duty; be this our prayer, to do it well."

We have seen, then, that we have every reason to confess that our times are in God's hand: One, we don't know the tomorrow; and two, the ephemeral nature of our life. As we now move on in our text, James suggests several ways in which we can affirm this conviction that our times are in God's hand.

Affirming This Personal Conviction

By Submitting to the Lord's Will

Instead you ought say, "If the Lord wishes, we will live and do this or that" (James 4:15). I recall that when I was a lad, a young man gave me his card on which he announced that he would be leaving for missionary work in India on a given date, D.V. I was puzzled at the letters D.V. and wondered what they might stand for. They are, as you may know, the abbreviation of the Latin *Deo volente* (God willing). It is a longstanding custom of Christian people to add D.V. at the end of letters or announcements regarding future plans. Sadly, this custom has fallen away. Not that it is always necessary for us to say "If the Lord wills" whenever we make a projection or a plan. But it would be fitting for us to say it more frequently. And certainly D.V. ought to be in our minds when we look into the future.

I am aware of the fact that the phrase "if the Lord wills" is used also among non-Christians. One thinks immediately of the Arabic *inshallah*, so common among Muslims. Some Jewish rabbis insisted that the formula "if the Lord wills" be used before any enterprise. In ancient religions, too, the gods were often consulted before decisions were taken, to avoid any suspicion of pride.

However, we are not thinking at the moment of the non-Christian use of the formula, nor of the perfunctory Christian use of it, but of the sincere and meaningful acknowledgment that our lives are in the hand of God.

Listen to Paul as he makes plans to go to Corinth: "I will come to you soon, if the Lord wills" (1 Cor. 4:19). "I hope to spend some time with you, if the Lord permits" (1 Cor. 16:7). Not all of his plans were realized. He writes to Timothy, "I hope to come to you soon, but I am writing these instructions to you so that, if I am delayed, you may know how one ought to behave in the household of God" (1 Tim. 3:14-15).

Helmut Gollwitzer, a young German theologian, was captured by the Russians at the end of World War II and was taken away to Siberia to a slave-labor camp. All through the years of suffering, his prayer was that of Teresa of Avila: "I am thine. What is your will for me?" In the midst of the suffering and despair, such a prayer took on meanings he had never thought of before.

Years ago I was deeply moved when I read the autobiography of the great Yale historian, Kenneth Scott Latourette, who had entitled his story *My Guided Life*.

Let us affirm the conviction we have that our times are in God's hand by submitting to the Lord's will. In the darkness of Gethsemane, the Savior prayed, "Not what I want, but what you want" (Mark 14:36). These words must become and remain the pattern for our lives. Let us also affirm this conviction by acknowledging God's providence in our lives.

Acknowledging God's Providence

If the Lord wishes, we will live and do this or that" (James 4:15). Older translations at times rendered our text in this way: "If the Lord wills and we live, then we shall do this or that." Thus Luther had it in his German version: "So der Herr will, und wir leben, wollen wir dies oder das tun." The better rendering, however, is: "If the Lord wills, we shall live and do this or that." The difference is considerable, for not only our future plans rest on God's providence, but our very life depends on it. We will live only if God wills.

God is the giver of life; God is the sustainer of life. We do not know how many days God will give us. Our life may suddenly come to an end. We live only by the grace and mercy of God. "When you take away their breath, they die and return to their dust" (Ps. 104:29). So we must receive every day as a gift from the patient and loving hand of our heavenly Father and ask for his blessing on every minute. It's comforting to know that the tiny stretches of my daily journey are just as important to God as the light years that measure the reaches of cosmic space.

By Repudiating All Sinful Pride
As it is, you boast in your arrogance; all such boasting is evil" (James 4:16). The Greek word *alazoneia* (bragging) is found as a noun only here and once more in 1 John 2:16, where it is usually translated as "the pride in riches." The NIV gives it there as "the boasting of what he has and does." The Greek *alazōn* is the word for a windbag, an arrogant, boastful braggart.

The Greeks had another word to describe human arrogance: *hybris*, which has come into English. This sin, said the ancients, was always punished by the gods. Hybris, they said, drove people to insane excesses of pride and insolence. Then in turn, Nemesis brought down the punishment of heaven upon the arrogant. That's the story of humankind in a nutshell.

C. S. Lewis writes that when he turned from atheism to

Christ in his later life, he began to be introspective and to examine his thoughts. To his friend, Greeves, in 1930, he confessed that pride was his besetting sin. "I have found out ludicrous and terrible things about my own character. Sitting by, watching the rising thoughts to break their necks as they pop up, one learns to know the sort of thoughts that do come. And, will you believe it, one out of every three is a thought of self-admiration. . . . It's like fighting the hydra. . . . There seems to be no end to it. . . . I am an instrument strung, but preferring to play itself because it thinks it knows the tune better than the Musician."

I am sure we have no difficulty identifying with Lewis, but by God's grace, we want to repudiate our sinful pride and live humbly before our God, confessing with the biblical writer: "My times are in your hand."

So as we reflect on our life, our Christian life, in this year that has run its course, we must confess that we have sometimes felt secure in ourselves. Often we made plans and decisions without prayer; we acted rather independently of God. So often we forgot about our human limitations; we forgot that our life was ephemeral in nature and that it quickly passes away.

Let us confess our many failures, confess that we have followed too much the devices and desires of our own heart, as the old prayer has it. We want to commit ourselves to God anew and submit our wills to God's will. We want to repudiate all sinful pride and arrogance and put our trust in the loving providence of our God.

4. New Year

The Promise of an Acceptable Year of the Lord

When he came to Nazareth, where he had been brought up, he went to the synagogue on the sabbath day, as was his custom. He stood up to read, and the scroll of the prophet Isaiah was given to him. He unrolled the scroll and found the place were it was written:
"The Spirit of the Lord is upon me,
  because he has anointed me
    to bring good news to the poor.
He has sent me to proclaim release
    to the captives
  and recovery of sight to the blind,
    to let the oppressed go free,
to proclaim the year of the Lord's favor
  [KJV: the acceptable year of the Lord]."
And he rolled up the scroll, gave it back to the attendant, and sat down. The eyes of all in the synagogue were fixed on him. Then he began to say to them, "Today this scripture has been fulfilled in your hearing."   (Luke 4:16-21)

We stand at the threshold of a new year. The month of January has just begun. January comes from the name of the old Roman god, Janus, who was represented as having two faces, one facing forward and the other facing backward. It is an appropriate name for the first month of our calendar. Quite naturally we look back over the year that has just passed.

All of us have had some troubles and trials in the past year, but we have survived. We needn't have. There may have been times when we even wondered whether we would make it through or not. Those were those dark moments when, perhaps, we felt like giving up. But God sustained us, and we are here today because of his mercy.

As we look back over the past year, we are keenly aware of our many failures. There were times when we chose the wrong road. Time and again we failed in love. Too often we followed the desires of our own hearts. Thus we have to plead God's forgiving grace.

But there were also many joyous occasions. We met people who enriched our lives. There were moments when we felt God was particularly close to us. We enjoyed many material gifts—health, freedom, and our daily sustenance. There were the joys of family life, and countless other blessings that came our way so undeservedly. And so we reflect with gratitude on the year that has slipped by.

Now we face a new year. Every year has surprises—some of them pleasant, others tragic and painful. But whatever may happen to us in the coming year, we know that it will be a *year of the Lord's favor* (NRSV), an *acceptable year of the Lord* (KJV). That is what Jesus promised his listeners on that very memorable Sabbath day when he came back to Nazareth, his hometown, in which he had grown up.

The synagogue leader had granted him the privilege of reading the lesson from the prophets and to give the homily. On this occasion our Lord read from the prophet Isaiah, who had announced hundreds of years ago that the sufferings of God's people were to come to an end and that *the acceptable year of the Lord* was about to begin. That promise was now to be fulfilled in a new way in the person and ministry of God's Messiah, Jesus the Christ. For when our Lord finished the reading of this promise, he added, *Today this Scripture has been fulfilled in your hearing.*

But what did Jesus mean when he claimed that he had come to proclaim the acceptable year of the Lord? Acceptable to whom? Acceptable to man? Is there such a thing as an unacceptable year? Do we have a choice? Such questions reflect a basic misunderstanding of our text.

If you have a more recent version of the Bible in your hands, you will probably have something like this: *To proclaim the year of the Lord's favor.* It is not a question of whether the year which Jesus announced in the synagogue of Nazareth is acceptable to man; rather, it is a proclamation that a year of grace is dawning, a year in which God's favor is shown toward those who don't really deserve it.

When Isaiah the prophet or Jesus spoke of *the acceptable year,* they were not thinking of a particular year, a year on our calendar, the year of Christ's birth,[1] for example, or the year in which Christ began his ministry.[2] Rather, it is the entire age of salvation. "See," writes Paul, "now is the acceptable time; see, now is the day of salvation" (2 Cor. 6:2).

Some early church fathers understood *the acceptable year of the Lord* to mean that Jesus served for one year only and then died and rose again and went to glory—all in one year. And from the first three Gospels, one could easily come to that conclusion. In the synoptic Gospels Jesus goes to Jerusalem only once, and that is to die. However, from John's Gospel we know that he went to Jerusalem for the Passover more than once, and so it is usually held that he ministered at least three years before he went to Jerusalem to die.

The expression *acceptable year* did, however, also have a

specific meaning in Old Testament times. It was the year of Jubilee, celebrated every fiftieth year in ancient Israel. This year was introduced by the blowing of the ram's horn. The ram's horn is called *jubal* in Hebrew, and that's where we get the word *Jubilee*. It was a year in which slaves were released; the land went back to its original owners; the impoverished were relieved of their debts. It was a year of forgiveness, called an *acceptable year* (Lev. 25:9; Isa. 61:2, KJV).

But when our Lord announced the arrival of the acceptable year of the Lord, he had something much more profound in mind. What he meant was that the age of salvation had dawned. That promise of Jesus, made almost two thousand years ago, still stands firm as the rock of Gibraltar. It awaits fulfillment once again in the coming year. Let us ponder anew Jesus' promise of an acceptable year of the Lord.

Who Makes This Promise?

Jesus of Nazareth

When he came to Nazareth, where he had been brought up (Luke 4:16). Although Jesus had made Capernaum by the Sea of Galilee the center of his ministry, he is never called "Jesus of Capernaum." He will always be "Jesus of Nazareth." When he died on a cruel cross, Pilate had the words written in mockery on a tablet above him, "Jesus of Nazareth, the King of the Jews" (John 19:19).

It was to Nazareth, to an insignificant village girl named Mary, that the angel Gabriel had come with the announcement that she would be the mother of the Messiah. To Nazareth Joseph and Mary returned with the baby Jesus after their flight to Egypt to escape the wrath of Herod the Great. Matthew observes that they settled in Nazareth so that the word spoken through the prophets might be fulfilled, "He will be called a Nazorean" or Nazarene (Matt. 2:23; cf. KJV).[3]

Our Lord had been to the Jordan just recently, where he had identified himself with sinful humanity and was baptized. And when he came out of the waters, he was endued with power from on high as the Spirit came down upon him. Immediately after his baptism, he went into the wilderness to be tested by the devil. There it became clear, once and for all, that he would go the path of obedience to his Father. He would not compromise; he would not flinch; he would do his Father's will. After the victory, Jesus returned in the power of the Spirit, and began his Galilean ministry. He was proclaiming the inbreaking of the kingdom of God, and his fame spread everywhere (Luke 4:14).

And now he is back home in Nazareth, and according to his custom he goes to the synagogue on the Sabbath. That incidental remark opens a tiny window on our Lord's life during the thirty years of silence, as he worked, apparently, as a carpenter, a builder, or craftsman (Mark 6:3). It was his custom to attend the synagogue. How we abhor custom nowadays! But good customs are some of the most liberating aspects of life. Eduard Schweizer of Zurich writes that good customs are like the railings along a stairway; they don't hinder us from going up and down, but they keep us from toppling over the edges.

But this morning something unusual happened in the synagogue of Nazareth. One of Nazareth's famous sons had come back home, and the ruler of the synagogue had asked him to read the Scriptures. The lessons from the Torah (five books of Moses) were fixed by now. It is not certain whether the lessons from the Prophets had already been fixed for each week of the year. Our text tells us only that he was given the book, the scroll of the prophet Isaiah, and that Jesus read from Isaiah 61:1-2. We do not know whether he chose that passage for this occasion or whether it was the prescribed reading for that day. Perhaps he was allowed to choose a reading within an allotted section.

We should keep in mind that Luke gives us only the reading from the Prophets and the homily that followed. There was much more to a synagogue service. It included the chanting or singing of one or more psalms, prayers, the recitation of the Shema,[4] and the lesson from the Torah (cf. Acts 13:14-43).

But Luke is writing a Gospel and is not giving us a complete description of a Jewish synagogue service. This is a book of good news and the good news is that Jesus of Nazareth on a memorable Sabbath day announced, in the presence of friends and relatives, that the acceptable year of the Lord had arrived. But we ask once again: Who makes this promise? The answer: The Anointed of the Lord.

The Anointed of the Lord

The Spirit of the Lord is upon me, because he has anointed me (Luke 4:18).   In Old Testament times, kings, priests, and even prophets were anointed with oil. Anointing meant at least two things: First, God had called and set a person apart for a particular kind of service. Second, God had given such persons the necessary equipment for this task. They were authorized, as it were, to carry on this service in God's name. The word *anoint* in the Hebrew is *mašiakh,* from which then comes our word Messiah. The Greek word for anoint is *chriō,* and from it comes the word *Christos,* Christ. So then, *Anointed, Messiah,* and *Christ* all mean the same thing.

All three Synoptists report that when Jesus was baptized and came up out of the water, the heavens were opened and the Holy Spirit came down upon him like a dove. This was in fulfillment of the promise about the branch that would spring from the root of David, upon whom God's Spirit would rest (Isa. 11:1-10). With the coming of the Spirit upon him, Jesus was equipped for his mission. Peter later recalls in the house of Cornelius how "God anointed Jesus of Nazareth with the Holy Spirit and with power; how he went about doing good and healing all who were oppressed by the devil, for God was with him" (Acts 10:38).

In John's Gospel we are told that when the Spirit came down upon Jesus at his baptism, the Spirit remained upon him (John 1:32). Jesus is the bearer of God's Spirit; he knows that he is the anointed of God, called and equipped to carry out the work of redemption. And so when he opens the book of Isaiah and begins to read, he begins with this overwhelming claim: *The Spirit of the Lord is upon me, because he has anointed me.* The promise of an acceptable year, then, comes first of all from Jesus of Nazareth; second, from the Anointed of God, the Messiah; and third, from God's Representative.

From God's Representative

Jesus, in applying the passage from Isaiah upon himself, makes the claim: *He has sent me* (Luke 4:18). God had sent him into this world as his representative. The verb to send is *apostellō* in Greek, from which we derive the word *apostle.* The writer to the Hebrews calls on his readers to consider Jesus, the apostle and high priest of our confession (Heb. 3:1).

When the residents of Capernaum wanted to keep Jesus in their town for themselves, that he might heal their sick, he said, No! I have to go to the other towns and villages to preach the gospel of the kingdom, "for I was sent for this purpose" (Luke 4:43). In the prayer of Jesus which he prayed in the shadow of the cross, he explained: "This is eternal life, that they may know you, the only true God, and Jesus Christ whom you have sent" (John 17:3).

Thus the promise of an acceptable year comes from God's representative, God's ambassador, who speaks with divine authority. This is not the prediction of some futurologist, who makes his annual forecasts; not from some palm-reader or fortune-teller or astrologist. This promise comes from one who came into the world at the midpoint of human history. One who by his death and resurrection established God's reign. One who is highly exalted today, waiting for the day when he will wrap up the present age and bring in the age to come.

An Acceptable Year: What Does This Promise Hold?

Good News for the Poor

To bring good news to the poor (Luke 4:18). Who are the poor? One answer: the economically poor. Then the rich are shut out. Is there, then, no good news for the well-to-do? If we think strictly in economic terms, what standard do we apply to establish who is rich and who is poor? Do we compare ourselves with the average American or the average Ethiopian? We get ourselves into a corner if we think of *poor* strictly in economic terms.

In the Old Testament *poor* came to be synonymous with godliness and genuine piety. The rich king David confesses, "This poor soul cried, and was heard by the Lord" (Psalm 34:6). He meant the godly person who puts trust in God. Jesus spoke a beatitude on the "poor in spirit," the humble, the obedient, those who put their hope and confidence in God, regardless of whether they are economically destitute or well-to-do (Matt. 5:3).

For those who do not look to themselves and their own resources for their salvation, the acceptable year of the Lord promises good news. Poverty of earthly goods doesn't save anybody; the poor and the affluent have to be redeemed by the death and resurrection of Jesus. The wealthy are also in need of divine help, and if they put their confidence in God, they can also be classified as poor in the presence of God.

Stephen Travis, an English theologian, writes in his book, *I Believe in the Second Coming of Jesus,* "In the Isaiah 61 passage the term 'poor' is explained by a whole series of parallel phrases: 'broken-hearted,' 'captives,' 'those in prison,' 'all who mourn.' " He goes on to say that "the poor are those who, because they are helpless, cast themselves on God's mercy, because they have nowhere else to go. They are 'empty' and therefore open to what God might do for them." [5]

If understood in this way, the good news is for all of us. None may trust in their own ability, expertise, cleverness, goodness, or righteousness for salvation. We all know that before God we all are sinners who have no hope of deliverance from sin and death and judgment—except through the grace of God in all its depth and fullness. The acceptable year of the Lord promises us the good news of salvation.

That was the message of the angel when Christ was born: "Do not be afraid; for see—I am bringing you good news of great joy for all the people," and we have just celebrated that great event (Luke 2:10).

There may be some reader who has heard the gospel many times over. You have gotten used to it, and your heart is as hard as the road in the parable of the sower (Mark 4:4). When the seed of God's Word falls upon your heart, it does not take root any more. Let this coming year be for you the acceptable year of the Lord. It's the year of God's favor. He's extending his grace to you. It's a good year of good news.

What else does the promise of an acceptable year of our Lord hold for us?

Freedom for Captives

He has sent me to proclaim release to the captives (Luke 4:18). When the prophet Isaiah spoke these words hundreds of years earlier, he had in mind the Israelites exiled in Babylon. His message to the captives was that one day they would again be free. The time would come when their exile, their bondage, would cease.

The word for *captive* in our text means quite specifically captives of war, people who have been swallowed up by an enemy of superior strength, as was the case when the Babylonians overwhelmed Judah. In Judaism it was considered highly meritorious to help prisoners of war, often the most wretched people on earth.

Here then is Jesus in the synagogue of Nazareth, picking up this hope of the prophet, announcing that the acceptable year of the Lord will bring liberty to captives. But who is meant by the captives? Rome took many captives in Palestine. Is he thinking of captive Jews, now in the hands of the Romans? Hardly! John the Baptist was in prison, but Jesus did not send John's disciples back to tell him that he would be released from jail.

This doesn't mean that prisoners do not need to hear the good news of the gospel. We thank God for those who minister to prisoners. But our Lord has an even greater bondage in mind. It is the bondage of sin and evil. It is the enslavement of the human will to the devil. And this strikes very close to home. This includes you and me—so often in the bondage of our egos, our selfishness.

The message of the angel to Joseph was that Mary would bear a child and they would call his name Jesus "for he will save his people from their sins" (Matt. 1:21). The very name *Jesus* (a Greek form of the Hebrew *Joshua*) means deliverer, savior, one who frees. Paul says he gave himself for us so that he might "set us free from the present evil age" (Gal. 1:4)—from its false values, idolatries, fears, and sins.

The writer to the Hebrews explains that Christ came to deliver those who through fear of death were subject to lifelong bondage (Heb. 2:15). And John writes from Patmos, dedicating his book "to him who loves us and freed us from our sins by his blood" (Rev. 1:5). A freedom train runs right through the Bible, inviting us to step in. Years ago in C. F. Henry's book *Unshackled*, I read stories of men and women who had been delivered from the dreadful bondage of sin into the freedom of the children of God.

And this doesn't happen all at once at conversion. This is an ongoing process. Through repentance, confession, and the mysterious working of the Holy Spirit in our lives, our bonds are loosed, we are unshackled, we are set free. Free, not to follow our own selfish desires, but free to serve God, free to walk in confidence and trust, free to love and to live with a conscience that no longer condemns.

Light for the Blind

And recovery of sight to the blind (Luke 4:18). Here Luke follows the Septuagint rather than the Hebrew of Isaiah 61. The Hebrew reads, "An opening for those in prison." The Greek translators evidently took the opening of the doors of the dark dungeon in which the prisoners sat to mean an opening of the eyes, for now they could again see daylight.

In the prophecy of Zechariah, the hope is expressed that a new day shall dawn from on high "to give light to those who sit in darkness and in the shadow of death" (Luke 1:79). When Jesus began his ministry in Galilee, Matthew saw in that the fulfillment of the prophetic word, "The people who sat in darkness have seen a great light, and for those who sat in the region and shadow of death light has dawned" (Matt. 4:16).

In his ministry of healing, our Lord did from time to

time heal blind people, quite literally, but the blindness of which our text speaks is of a different sort. The light which Christ promises to give to the blind is not natural eyesight, not 20/20 vision. No, it is the light of salvation.

Satan, writes Paul, "has blinded the minds of the unbelievers, to keep them from seeing the light of the gospel of the glory of Christ" (2 Cor. 4:4). And he compares the new birth with creation. "The God who said, 'Let light shine out of darkness' . . . has shone in our hearts to give the light of the knowledge of the glory of God in the face of Jesus Christ" (2 Cor. 4:6). This is well expressed in the hymn: "Out of my bondage, sorrow and night . . . Into thy freedom, gladness and light . . . Jesus, I come to thee" (W. T. Sleeper).

Paul speaks of the eyes of our hearts being enlightened (Eph. 1:18). Our hearts have shutters, and they need to be opened to let the light of God shine in. Paul says that a veil hangs over the minds of unbelieving Israel when they read the Scriptures, and only when they put their trust in Christ is that veil removed so that they can see (2 Cor. 3:15-16). Christ the Word, "the true light, which enlightens everyone, was coming into the world," writes John (1:9). One of the most overwhelming claims Jesus ever made was "I am the light of the world" (John 8:12).

We have just come through the Christmas season, celebrated with a great array of lights. Our Advent songs also are pervaded with this theme: "Come to the Light, 'tis shining for thee; Sweetly the Light has dawned upon me, Once I was blind, but now I can see: the Light of this world is Jesus" (P. P. Bliss).

As I prepared this message, I looked at my bookshelf and there stood the volume by Emile Cailliet, French philosopher become Christian theologian, who wrote the story of his conversion under the title, *Journey into Light*.

How blind we are! We do not know as we should. We

don't understand ourselves properly; we don't see other people as we should. Often we are so blind to what God is doing in the world, in the church. In matters of right and wrong, we often have poor eyesight. As we enter upon a new year, we have the promise of a year of the Lord's favor, and that includes the promise of light for our way. "Whoever follows me," said Jesus, "will never walk in darkness but will have the light of life" (John 8:12).

Help for the Broken

To let the oppressed go free (Luke 4:18). The Greek verb *thrauō* gives us the English word *trauma* and means broken, battered, bruised, oppressed, downtrodden.

What has always puzzled Bible readers is that Jesus wove this line from Isaiah 58:6 into the reading of the passage from Isaiah 61. Did Jesus roll back the scroll, reading excerpts from a block of chapters? Had some scribe written this line in the margin of Isaiah 61 as a cross-reference? Was he reading from a lectionary? We do not know, but here we have it now in Luke's Gospel. In the acceptable year of the Lord, Christ promises to stand by the traumatized, the broken and beaten and bruised.

Joseph Parker, great preacher of London, England, advised fellow ministers always to preach to broken hearts. In every congregation, he insisted, there are those whose hearts cry out for healing. Even in the lives of those who are healthy, successful, and prosperous, those who have made it, as we say, there is always some pain, some brokenness, some trauma. That's part of our life here on earth. Even as Christians we enjoy only the firstfruits of the Holy Spirit. Fullness of life and perfection lie in the world to come. In the words of Paul, we groan inwardly as we wait for the redemption of the body (Rom. 8:23; 2 Cor. 5:4).

There is so much in the world that causes us pain. Our daily work at times brings with it all kinds of unpleasantries. The life of the church is often not what we might wish. Family life, with all its joys, is often attended by quiet sorrow, and in our personal life we are often crushed, bruised, and broken.

But Christ promises to help us in our brokenness. He won't leave us to ourselves, he won't abandon us. The psalmist writes that even "if I make my bed in Sheol, you are there" (Ps. 139:8). Lewis Smedes, professor at Fuller Seminary, writes in one of his books about the many mini-hells into which we fall, only to discover that even there, God is with us.

So then let the brokenhearted make their way to Jesus. No sorrow is outside the compass of his help. He comes to tormented hearts in the hour of their need and holds them firmly in his hand in the tempests of life. How tenderly he deals with those for whom life has been darkened by disappointments. He meets us on the way to Jericho, when we lie half-dead beside the road, and pours oil and wine into our wounds. Help for the broken! That knowledge alone should make the coming year an acceptable year of the Lord.

An Acceptable Year: How Do We Respond to This Promise?

How Did the Original Listeners Respond?

At first they are awestruck; they are quite overwhelmed by *words of such grace* (Luke 4:22, REB). But quickly their attitude changes. Why, isn't this Joseph's son? Who does he think he is, making such claims? They are likely offended that Jesus stops reading just before the proclamation of "the day of vengeance of our God" (Isa. 61:2). They want punishment for the Gentiles.

Jesus immediately senses their unsympathetic attitude and explains that the people of Nazareth, his friends, and his relatives are repeating the story of Israel in days of old, when they refused to accept the prophet Elijah. Then God sent him to a Sidonian widow, who cared for him (Luke 4:26).

And Elijah's successor, Elisha, healed the leper Naaman, the Syrian, but none of the lepers in Israel (Luke 4:27). In effect Jesus is saying, in the past, when Israel rejected the words of the prophets, God sent them to non-Israelites, to Gentiles, and that's what will happen again. The openness of foreigners to the prophets contrasts with the resistance of Nazareth to Jesus' proclamation of the year of the Lord's favor.

Yet God has no favorites. God wants all people to be saved and to come to the knowledge of the truth (1 Tim. 2:4). But when people reject the truth, God passes them by. God breaks out the natural branches, Israel, and grafts wild branches, the Gentiles, into the Abrahamic tree. Why? Because Israel rejected the gospel, and the Gentiles received it (cf. Rom. 11:17-24).

The visitors in the synagogue on that memorable Sabbath morning, when Jesus announced the acceptable year of the Lord, were more privileged than others. But they allowed the day of salvation to pass by. In the end they take Jesus to a cliff with the evil intent of pushing him down in order to kill him (Luke 4:29). Nazareth had missed the hour of salvation, the acceptable year of our Lord.

And How Do We Respond?

Are we going to say, What else is new? We've heard all that before. Yes, you are right, for the gospel is two thousand years old, and we can't invent a new gospel. All we can do is to cast it in new forms so that the old gospel becomes a fresh word from God for us. And that can happen only if the Holy Spirit gives us open ears to hear the message once again.

For those who have heard the good news many times

but have never responded in faith and obedience, let the coming year be the acceptable year of the Lord. Let this be the year of forgiveness, the year of liberation from the bondage of guilt and fear and evil powers. "Now is the acceptable time; see, now is the day of salvation!" (2 Cor. 6:2).

5. Lent

The Wonder of Redemption

*Grace to you and peace from God our Father and the Lord
Jesus Christ, who gave himself for our sins to set us free
from the present evil age, according to the will of our God
and Father, to whom be the glory forever and ever. Amen.*

(Gal. 1:3-5)

Jesus *gave himself for our sins.* That's the gospel in a nutshell. That's the message of the cross that had changed the
lives of the Galatians. In Galatians 3:1 Paul reminds them
of those early days when Christ "was publicly exhibited as
crucified." The saving gospel which Paul preached is
called "the message about the cross" (1 Cor. 1:18). By
Christ's death on the cross, we were delivered from our
sins.

Paul himself had held out against the cross for so long.
Indeed, he had tried to destroy those who believed in a
crucified Messiah, for a Messiah who hung upon a tree
was an abomination to the Jews. Deuteronomy 21:23
plainly stated that anyone who hung upon a tree was
cursed of God—a text which Paul quotes in Galatians 3:13.

However, all this changed on the Damascus Road when
Paul discovered that the one who had suffered such a
shameful death on the cross was alive. If so, then by raising

Jesus from the dead, God clearly had reversed the judgment of the Jewish Sanhedrin and of the Roman governor. Jesus was then not under the curse of God but under divine favor. He had died not for his own sins but for ours. He became a curse for us.

Once Paul had encountered the risen Christ on the way to Damascus, he had but one passion: to preach Christ and him crucified. "May I never boast of anything except the cross of our Lord Jesus Christ," he writes to the Galatians (6:14). And when Paul came to Corinth, he resolved to know nothing among them except Christ and him crucified (1 Cor. 2:1-4). For Paul, the cross is the center of sacred history; it takes in the entire sweep of the story of redemption.

From the vantage point of the cross and the resurrection, the Old Testament was seen in a new light. From the cross the New Testament writers looked into the future and saw the triumph of God at the end of the age, not by the clash of arms but by the Lamb that was slain. But not only does the past take on new meaning; not only does the future burn more brightly; the present also takes on a new character. Through the deliverance from sin, God's people are now enabled "in the present age to live lives that are ... godly" (Tit. 2:12).

The cross early became the key Christian symbol in art and architecture. Other religions may have the crescent, the lotus flower, the sun's disk, the flame, but Christianity is unique. It has a cross. And the reason: Jesus *gave himself for our sins to set us free.* The Christian gospel offers deliverance from sin, and that was made possible when Christ died on the cross.

Paul uses a great many figures of speech to proclaim the message of redemption. He speaks of being ransomed—a metaphor from the realm of slavery. We have been justified—a word from the lawcourt. We have been purchased

—an economic term. And then there are the many expressions from the realm of Israel's sacrificial system—expiation, propitiation, and so forth. So rich and wonderful was the good news of redemption that Paul ransacked his vocabulary, as it were, to bring out its many facets. In our passage, redemption is seen as a rescue, a deliverance. *He gave himself for our sins that he might free us.*

We will never fully understand the mystery of what happened when Christ gave himself for our sins. Thus it is quite appropriate to speak of the "wonder of redemption." Let me point out some of the facets of this glorious message from Galatians 1:3-5.

The Need for Redemption

The need for redemption is suggested by the expression *our sins.* In order to appreciate the message of deliverance, we must take seriously what the Bible calls *sin.* Light thoughts on sin lead to light thoughts on redemption. The gospel is good news for those who have come to see that they need to be delivered from their sins.

The word sin (Greek: *hamartia*) was not too serious a term in everyday Greek usage. It simply meant failure of some sort—missing the mark, going astray, failing to come up to some standard. But when the word was taken up by the biblical writers, it came to denote a violation of God's holy laws, perversity, disobedience, rebellion against the Almighty.

The entire history of humankind is united in its witness to the awful reality of sin in the lives of men and women. There is no page in the history of humanity that has been left unstained by sin. Not only do God's Word and human history testify to the grim fact that the power of sin is at work in human lives, but our own consciences also witness to this "gravitational pull" in our lives. It is that evil power that perverts our good desires, darkens our minds, enslaves our wills, and causes so much wretchedness and disorder in our lives.

Some have wanted to remove the concept of sin from Christian vocabulary. It was an unseemly word, they thought. At best, it described our growing pains. To call someone a sinner was to deny the goodness of human beings, or at least, their perfectibility. Gresham Machen, founder of Westminster Seminary, tells of a minister who led in public prayer and caught himself quoting Jeremiah 17:9 (KJV): "The heart is deceitful above all things, and desperately wicked." He quickly added, "And, Lord, you know this is no longer true." But the awful tragedies of this enlightened, twentieth century take us back to biblical realism with respect to our fallenness. We had better not pretend to be wiser than God. Let us acknowledge our need for deliverance from sin.

James Packer writes: "To say that our first need in life is to learn about sin may sound strange, but in the sense intended, it is profoundly true. If you have not learned about sin, you cannot understand yourself or your [fellows], or the world you live in, or the Christian faith. And you will not be able to make head or tail of the Bible." [1]

During the Protestant Reformation, some mystics held that there was a divine spark hidden deep down in the human heart (cf. Plato). If this were fanned into flame, a person might raise oneself up and come closer to God. But Luther rejected this mysticism by declaring that deep in the center of our being we are rebels against God. The mystics had simply not looked deep enough. And in his conflict with Erasmus the humanist, he wrote the book, *The Bondage of the Will,* in which he stressed not only human sinfulness but also our blindness that keeps us from seeing our true condition.

Back in the fourth century, a monk by the name of Pelagius taught that human nature was basically neutral.

Human beings suffer only from bad examples. Every individual begins life with a clean slate. Others thought that a bit too optimistic, for there is in all human beings the tendency toward evil. The theologian Augustine understood the Bible to say that humans are dead in trespasses and sins, and unless new life is infused, they are lost (Eph. 2:1, 5).

And that is the message of our text: Jesus gave himself to deliver us from our sins. The passage speaks not only of the need of redemption but also of the method: *He gave himself.*

The Method of Redemption

To deliver us from our sins Jesus *gave himself.* He voluntarily surrendered his life. "I lay down my life . . . of my own accord," said Jesus (John 10:17-18). Paul also speaks of the voluntary surrender of Jesus' life. "Christ loved us and gave himself up for us" (Eph. 5:2). And Peter chimes in: "He himself bore our sins in his body on the cross" (1 Pet. 2:24).

That's another way of saying that salvation is entirely of grace. God takes the initiative and sacrifices his Son. Deliverance comes to us as a gift. We cannot deliver ourselves from the bondage of sin. Christ gave himself *for our sins.* That suggests that his death was a vicarious sacrifice. He died for our sake. He is "the Lamb of God who takes away the sin of the world!" (John 1:29).

Every day sacrifices were brought in the temple in Jerusalem, and the lamb had already become the symbol of substitutionary death. Since the priest participated in these sacrificial rites, the priest himself had become a symbol of vicarious sacrifice. Therefore, the writer to the Hebrews can say that our Lord is "a merciful and faithful high priest . . . to make a sacrifice of atonement for the sins of the people" (Heb. 2:17). The shedding of the blood of innocent victims underscored the concept of vicarious sacrifice in the thinking of the Jew. It is not surprising, then, that the apostles relate the deliverance from sin to the blood that Christ shed on Calvary. Christ "loves us and freed us from our sins by his blood" (Rev. 1:5). "In him we have redemption through his blood, the forgiveness of our trespasses" (Eph. 1:7). "Christ loved us and gave himself up for us, a fragrant offering and sacrifice to God" (Eph. 5:2).

C. S. Lewis warned against arguing over the best way to describe the atonement. Some people say that Christ paid the debts we owed, or he suffered the punishment we earned. Some say he washed us in his blood; others, that he conquered. "However one states it," says Lewis, "it was something no one less than God could do. And it hurt." [2]

Jesus *gave himself for our sins . . . according to the will of our God and Father.* That suggests that Christ's saving death was in the plan of God. It was not an accident; it was not an unforeseen event. Christ was "the Lamb slain from the foundation of the world" (Rev. 13:8, KJV). Although his disciples could at first not comprehend how the death of Jesus could be part of his redemptive mission, later, after the resurrection, it all became clear to them. All this happened "according to the definite plan and foreknowledge of God," said Peter in his Pentecost sermon (Acts 2:23).

"You were ransomed," Peter writes in his first letter, "not with perishable things like silver or gold, but with the precious blood of Christ, like that of a lamb without defect or blemish. He was destined before the foundation of the world" (1 Pet. 1:18-20).

One of the central truths of the gospel, according to Paul's summary in 1 Corinthians (15:3-8), is that "Christ died for our sins in accordance with the scriptures." Although the cross is not mentioned in the Old Testament (yet cf. Gal. 3:13; Deut. 21:23), the apostles thought of the

Jewish Scriptures as anticipating the death of Jesus (as in Isa. 52:13—53:12). There was a cross in the heart of God long before there was a cross on Calvary's mountain.

This was strongly contested by Marcion in the second century. He rejected the Old Testament, saying it revealed a different God from that of the New Testament. But he was wrong. It was the God of Abraham, Isaac, and Jacob, who gave his only Son for the salvation of the world (John 3:16). "He who did not withhold his own Son, but gave him up for all of us, will he not with him also give us everything else?" (Rom. 8:32). "Thanks be to God for his indescribable gift!" (2 Cor. 9:15). "By the grace of God [Jesus did] taste death for everyone" (Heb. 2:9).

I am told that in the National Art Gallery in London there is a picture of the Crucified. At first one notices only the figure of Jesus on the cross. On closer examination, however, more begins to emerge out of the darkness—the dim outlines of another head behind Christ's head, other arms behind his arms, other legs behind his legs. God was suffering there in his Son. According to the will of God, he gave himself for our sins to deliver us.

Richard Holloway describes the wonder of redemption in this way:

> Mankind is a land fallen into enemy hands. We belong to God, but his rule has been usurped by the great enemy of God, the devil, the prince of this world, who now holds us in bondage. We are not free to serve God, free to be good, free to love, free to be our true selves, free not to die. We are slaves, bound under the heel of this tyrant, the devil.
>
> And then Christ the Liberator comes forth from God, like a commando from the Almighty. . . . He comes right into enemy territory and begins a campaign of sabotage as he casts out demons, the devil's servants.

He gathers round him a guerrilla army, his disciples, whom he trains for the mopping-up operations that will follow his great battle.

Then he moves toward the final showdown: he takes on Death itself, that great sign of the dominion of the devil. He submits to death and so destroys it from within. In hand-to-hand combat he breaks the very rule of death, shattering its grisly power over men and women. The final sign of that victory is the Resurrection: that's when he hoists the colors of God over his wounded creation; the devil is routed and taken captive, and death and sin and the shedding of eternal tears is stopped forever.[3]

In prose, poetry, and hymnody, Christians throughout the centuries have testified to the liberation from sins which Christ secured by his death. "I lay in fetters groaning, Thou cam'st to set me free."

The strife is o'er, the battle done;
Now is the Victor's triumph won;
Now be the song of praise begun.
    Alleluia!   *(Anonymous 17th-century Latin hymn)*

Our passage, however, speaks not only of the need for redemption, and the method of redemption, but also of its unique purpose.

The Unique Purpose

Who gave himself for our sins to set us free from the present evil age (Gal. 1:4). The verb *to set free* or *deliver* (Greek: *exaireō*) speaks of a rescue operation. It is used to describe Israel's rescue from the clutches of Pharaoh (Acts 7:34), Peter's rescue from prison (Acts 12:11), Paul's rescue from an angry mob (Acts 23:27). We have been emancipated from a state of bondage.

But what does Paul mean when he speaks of deliverance from the present evil age? In Jewish thought there were only two ages: the present, which was dark and evil; and the future, bright and glorious. In time the word *age* took on an ethical meaning alongside its temporal meaning. It spoke of the character and spirit of the age—something like the German word *Zeitgeist*. In Ephesians 2:2 Paul speaks of the "age" or "course of this world." He does not mean the antiquity of this world but the temper, the spirit, the ways of this world. And this present age is described as evil in our text. We have been rescued from this present evil spirit of the world.

From a temporal point of view, we are still much in this present age. Eternity has not yet begun for us. We have temporal and physical needs; we are caught up in the bundle of life here on this earth (1 Sam. 25:29). We are subject to pain, to disaster, to death. We have unfulfilled longings. Yet from a moral point of view, we have been freed from this present age. We are no longer in bondage to the values, the emptiness, the hopes, the futility, the pleasures of this age.

Early Christian writers repeatedly testify to the liberation which Christ has brought them through the gospel. Justin Martyr, who laid down his life for his Christian witness, was asked by a Roman trial judge, "Who are you?" Justin answered, "I am a Christian, having been set at liberty by Christ." And he was condemned to death. Tatian, another second-century Christian, in his *Address to the Greeks*, praises Christ for having rescued him from the bondage of evil, condemnation, and error, and the thousand tyrants that had formerly dominated his life. In the eighteenth century Charles Wesley is still singing the song of freedom: "My chains fell off, my soul is free, for thou my God did'st die for me."

Christ died also to deliver us from divine wrath and

eternal condemnation, but our text speaks of an emancipation from this present evil age, that is, from worldliness. Final deliverance, including the redemption of the body, will be ours when Jesus returns, but deliverance from this present evil age is something we can experience even today. And all these blessings are summed up in two words, so familiar to us from the Pauline letters: Grace and peace.

The Spiritual Foundation

Our text is one sentence: *Grace to you and peace from God our Father and the Lord Jesus Christ, who gave himself for our sins to set us free from the present evil age, according to the will of our God and Father* (Gal. 1:3-4). The foundation for this wonderful work of redemption is to be found in God's grace and peace which have come to us through Jesus Christ.

The normal word of salutation at the beginning of a Greek letter was *rejoice*. By a small linguistic switch, Paul changes *chairein* (rejoice) to *charis* (grace). The normal word of salutation at the beginning of Jewish letter was *shalom* (peace). However, peace in Jewish thought was not simply the absence of strife. It included wholeness, well-being, salvation. Paul appears to combine the greetings of East and West, but he transforms and deepens them. Through Jesus Christ, God has manifested his grace and his salvation. Through Jesus, God opened up the fountains of saving grace, brought us freedom from sin and guilt and death, and emancipated us from this present evil age.

Grace and peace embrace all the blessings of salvation. These two words, which Paul has baptized into Christ, always stand in this order. When God's grace flows into our lives and we experience its liberating power, God's peace floods our souls. If grace is the fountain, then peace is the river that keeps on flowing, even as we travel through the wilderness of this world. And when the grace and the peace of God come into the lives of people who long for freedom, there is always a glad response. This is expressed in our passage by the doxology: "To whom be the glory forever and ever. Amen" (Gal. 1:5).

The Personal Response

P. T. Forsyth, a Congregationalist theologian, points out that Christ's death does not bring a spontaneous response of honor, love, and gratitude, in contrast with praise heaped on heroes dying for their country. The reason, says Forsyth, is that he, Jesus, died *for our sins,* and the response to such a death calls for repentance.[4] And so we will have to admit that God's gift of grace includes even the personal response of the soul that has been set free from bondage.

Those who have experienced the wonder of redemption in their lives have a desire to give Christ glory for ever and ever. They give him glory by worshiping him. They give him back the gift of their lives. They serve him, seek God's kingdom and righteousness, and remain loyal and true to Christ. They order their lives so that Christ is glorified. Even eating and drinking is done to the glory of God (1 Cor. 10:31).

Edwin and his girlfriend Hilda knew of the cross and the redemption that was accomplished on Calvary, but that now meant nothing to them. The wonder of redemption had faded from their lives. One day they stumbled upon a Sunday school pageant being performed in a midwestern town of the United Sates. At first they watched with derision and pity for people who still believed in that kind of nonsense.

Then suddenly the children began to sing: "When I survey the wondrous cross, on which the Prince of glory died, my richest gain I count but loss, and pour contempt on all my pride." Hilda was deeply moved and she turned her face to hide her emotions. Edwin asked sharply: "What's the matter?" Hilda replied: "It would be worth anything in the world to say those words and to mean them."

Yes, indeed! To know the wonder of redemption is worth everything in this world!

6. Palm Sunday

Preparing for the Passion

Six days before the Passover Jesus came to Bethany, the home of Lazarus, whom he had raised from the dead. There they gave a dinner for him. Martha served, and Lazarus was one of those at the table with him. Mary took a pound of costly perfume made of pure nard, anointed Jesus' feet, and wiped them with her hair. The house was filled with the fragrance of the perfume. But Judas Iscariot, one of his disciples (the one who was about to betray him), said, "Why was this perfume not sold for three hundred denarii and the money given to the poor?" (He said this not because he cared about the poor, but because he was a thief; he kept the common purse and used to steal what was put into it.) Jesus said, "Leave her alone. She bought it so that she might keep it for the day of my burial. You always have the poor with you, but you do not always have me."　　　(John 12:1-8)

This passage marks the beginning of the passion narrative in John's Gospel. It is approximately in the middle of the Gospel. Obviously, when almost half a book is devoted to the death and resurrection of its chief character, we know where the interest of the writer lies. It is not surprising, then, that our Gospels have been described as passion stories with long introductions.

By comparison, in a 650-page biography of the great

Scottish preacher, Alexander Whyte, one sentence is devoted to his death. But in the Gospels, Christ's death is the central theme. The good news of the gospel is that Christ died for our sins.

The passion story in the Gospels is a powerful piece of writing. Sometimes one wishes one could read the story for the first time, in order to get the full impact. Familiarity has taken the edge off the narrative. But many unbelievers, on reading the story of Christ's death and resurrection for the first time, gave their lives over to Christ in response to this gripping story.

One illustration must suffice. Norman Snaith, famous Old Testament scholar and author of many books, was an agnostic in his college days. He had severed all ties with the church and religion as such. But then came the day when he turned to the New Testament and read the account of Christ's passion; God invaded his life, and he became a follower of the one who had suffered and died for him.

Turning then to our text, we notice that it was Passover season, and Jesus had come up to Jerusalem. Jesus spent most of his life in Galilee, but Old Testament prophets had foreseen the day when the good news of salvation would go forth from Jerusalem. So our Lord went to Jerusalem when his hour had come.

The road to Jerusalem was not an easy one to take. No person in his early thirties looks joyfully at the prospect of a cruel death. But, as Luke puts it, "when the days drew near for him to be taken up, he set his face to go to Jerusalem" (Luke 9:51). It was a lonely road. His disciples had not yet grasped the meaning of Christ's repeated predictions of his death.

In fact, Peter protested violently when Jesus talked about his sufferings and death (Mark 8:32). The disciples were still thinking of Messiah as a powerful political and military leader who would establish a national Jewish kingdom. The thought had not yet sunk into their minds that the Messiah should die and in that way establish his reign over the hearts and lives of his friends (John 15:14).

Before Jesus' arrival in Jerusalem, the Jewish leaders had put a price on his head (John 11:57). Before long one of his trusted followers, Judas, began to plan the betrayal of his Master to his enemies. But with great courage our Lord approached the Via Dolorosa, the way of sorrow.

By contrast to this ominous prospect, John slips in a delightful story of the anointing of Jesus in the house of friends. The story was considered so important that three of the four Gospels have it (Luke omits this account but has another anointing of Jesus, by a sinful woman off the street: Luke 7:36-50). There are both differences and similarities in the accounts of the anointing of Jesus before his death. For example, Matthew and Mark put the story after the triumphal entry into Jerusalem, while John places it before that symbolical act.

The anointing of Jesus was part of the preparation for his passion, and that is the topic of our message. The account focuses on three individuals: on Mary and her extravagant love, on Judas and his niggardly protest, and on Jesus and his profound interpretation of Mary's deed. Let us, then, retell the story and inquire into its message, as we look at these three personages in turn.

The Extravagance of Mary (John 12:1-3)

The Setting

It was six days before the Passover. Since in John that Passover was on the Sabbath, this scene would probably be on Saturday evening, after the Sabbath had come to a close, and it was lawful to prepare a meal. There was to be no work, such as the lighting of fires, on the Sabbath.

Jerusalem was crowded with visitors from all over the

Roman world. It is estimated that the population of the city quadrupled at this time of the year. The city was declared common property of all Jewry for this week, and that meant that lodging was not too much of a problem. Pentecost, fifty days later, was normally better attended than Passover, because travel on the Mediterranean was safer later in the spring. Yet at Passover messianic hopes coupled with nationalistic feelings always ran high, for at that festival Israel remembered the deliverance from Egyptian bondage.

Prudence would have counseled Jesus to stay away from Jerusalem with its seething masses at this time, or at least to slip into the city unseen and remain concealed in some of the back streets. But that was precisely what Jesus would not do. God's hour for him had struck. He had counted the cost, and with great courage he would walk into the very jaws of death.

It must have warmed our Lord's heart when they prepare a supper for him in the circle of intimate friends. Some of them must be seeing the dark storm clouds gathering around the Master's head.

Mark informs us that the supper is held in the home of Simon the Leper, who lives in Bethany. Certainly if he is still a leper, he would not live in Bethany. Moreover, he may have been one of the lepers whom Jesus healed but the nickname *the leper* stayed with him. Since Lazarus, Mary, and Martha are mentioned, it has been suggested that Simon is their father, but that is conjecture.

That Martha serves at the dinner is a delightful touch. At a former occasion when Jesus dined with the sisters, Martha complained that she was left alone with the dishes (Luke 10:38-42). But now with a much larger group to serve, she does so without grumbling.

How kind of these friends to open their hearts and their home to Jesus just before the cruel hatred of his enemies attempts to put out the light of life! We all know something of how safe we feel when we are with friends. In their midst we don't need to weigh our thoughts or measure our words. Friends can be trusted.

The Manner

Having looked at the setting in which Mary demonstrated her love, let us observe her manner. Jesus and his disciples are reclining at tables, a sign of a special occasion. Normally people sat when they partook of food. Standing was forbidden, for that was the sign of slavery. Once on Passover night in Egypt they had stood, ready for the Exodus. But now they were a free people, and so there was to be no standing. Reclining, however, was practiced only at festivals and formal occasions, when people lay on divans, leaning on their left arm and eating with the right.

As Jesus reclines with his friends, Mary comes from behind, carrying a small container made of alabaster, in which was concentrated perfume. Alabaster is the name for a flask with a long neck made of glassy marble. By sealing the flask, the fragrance is retained. A pound of this costly unguent made of nard could represent an enormous expense.

Mary comes from behind and anoints Jesus' feet with this expensive perfume and wipes his feet with her hair. Mark informs us that she breaks the flask, its neck, and pours out the entire contents on Jesus. Sometimes in those days when a famous person came to dinner, the goblet out of which he drank was later broken into fragments, so that no one else should ever drink from it. The donkey on which Jesus rode into Jerusalem was one on which no one had ever ridden. The tomb in which he was laid was one in which no other person had ever lain. It was a way of saying that he was very special.

Normally such perfume was poured on the head, and

indeed Mark tells us Mary also anointed his head. But John informs us that she anoints his feet, and then she wipes them with her hair instead of with a towel. That is all the more striking, since a Jewish woman never unbound her hair in public. It was then a most extraordinary manifestation of love and devotion. Anointing the head was part of etiquette and hospitality, but to anoint the feet was an unusual act of devotion.

The Motive

What may have moved Mary to manifest her love for Jesus in such an extravagant manner? We can never be quite sure when we talk about motives, for we cannot look into other people's hearts. But let us recall the several occasions at which Mary had an encounter with Jesus, as reported by the Gospel writers. We cannot help but feel that these experiences formed the background for her gracious deed.

In the previous chapter (John 11) we have the story of the raising of Lazarus from the dead, Mary's brother. Perhaps this is Mary's way of saying thanks. Or, if we go back a bit further to that memorable occasion when Jesus visited the sisters in their home in Bethany, we find Mary sitting at Jesus' feet and listening to his teachings (Luke 10:38-42). Perhaps she first grasped the truth that Jesus was Messiah while sitting "at his feet," a Semitic way of saying she was a disciple. In contrast to Jesus' disciples, she accepts the fact that Messiah must die (John 12:7). She may have saved for some time in order to purchase this costly perfume so that she could anoint her Master before he died.

We all know that there are moments in life which do not come a second time—impulses to change, decision, action. And if these opportunities are missed, they never return. There is an old Latin proverb that runs, "Whoever gives quickly, gives twice" (*qui cito dat dis dat*). A gift given at the right time is of double value. "Whenever we have an opportunity," writes Paul to the Galatians, "let us work for the good of all" (Gal. 6:10).

If we could look into Mary's mind, we might hear her asking herself as did the psalmist: "What shall I return to the Lord for all his bounty to me?" (Ps. 116:12). Mary seizes the moment and pours out her gratitude, love, and understanding.

There is a place in our giving for planning and for common sense. But we must not discount those impulses that lead us to some deed of kindness at the spur of the moment. The impulse to speak a gracious word, to write a letter of encouragement, to help someone in need.

Mary's act is so unsophisticated and artless. Without calculating the cost, she pours out her love, as it were. And the house is full of the fragrance—a fragrance which time cannot erase. To this day her devotion moves our hearts (Mark 14:9). An act of love is never simply a momentary thing. It always leaves a legacy behind. Dorcas with her needle will be remembered when Napoleon is forgotten. Mary with her alabaster box will be a living memory when Alexander the Great's name is buried in oblivion.

But now let us focus on the second person who plays a key role in this account: Judas.

The Reaction of Judas (John 12:4-6)

His Words of Protest

According to our text, Judas alone protests (John 12:5). But Matthew adds that the other disciples agree with him. Judas thinks that Mary's act is a fantastic waste. It is sheer recklessness.

With a sense of sadness, John characterizes Judas, his former fellow apostle. He says he was one of Jesus' disciples and that he was the one who is about to betray his

Master. He doesn't launch a tirade against the traitor but brings out the enormity of his guilt by setting these two observations side by side: a disciple and the one who betrays Jesus. What fathomless abyss of sin and wickedness is opened up to us in that paradoxical statement!

Judas's love for money enabled him quickly to calculate the cost of the "wasted" ointment. It could bring three hundred denarii. That's a year's wages, for laborers at that time received about a denarius a day. Yet Judas covered up his greed with a pious comment. The money could have been given to the poor.

Materialistically minded people often despise those who make sacrifices for the sake of the kingdom of God. Sometimes they are criticized for lacking business sense or not knowing the value of a dollar. But our God loves a *hilarious* giver, says Paul (2 Cor. 9:7, Greek).

When Albert Schweitzer decided to leave Europe and to devote the remainder of his life to Africa, Christian friends (including ministers) cautioned him against throwing away his great gifts and his learning. Trained in music, philosophy, and theology, he embarked upon medical training in order to serve Lazarus on the doorstep of affluent Europe. But, had he not thrown his life away, as some thought he did, we would probably know little about him today.

John's Words of Condemnation

Following Judas's word of protest against Mary's lavish gift, we have the Evangelist's word of condemnation (John 12:6). Writing long after Judas had perished, John says Judas really didn't care for the poor. It is the waste of three hundred denarii that disturbs him. He is actually a thief and is helping himself to the common purse, of which he is in charge. Hence, immediately after this incident in Bethany, Judas goes to the Jewish leaders and offers to betray Jesus for thirty pieces of silver. Seeing one sum of money lost, he hurries to find another. A mind twisted by avarice has little appreciation for costly deeds of love. Dante puts him in the lowest hell, the hell of ice and snow, reserved for cool, calculating, presumptuous sinners.

From Mary's expression of love and Judas's manifestation of greed, we turn now to the interpretation which Jesus puts on Mary's action. This interpretation is also a scathing criticism of Judas.

Jesus' Explanation (John 12:7-8; Mark 14:6-9)

Meaning for the Anointing

Jesus begins by giving meaning to the act of Mary (John 12:7). Jesus takes Mary's side. He will have nothing to do with the avaricious mentality of Judas. *Leave her alone,* is his command, and then he gives her act of love a profound significance.

He explains that Mary has anointed him for burial. He is fully aware of his impending death. He knows he's on the way to Calvary. Godly women will come to embalm his body after he dies, but then it is too late. He has arisen from the dead (Luke 23:55-56; 24:1-8). Mary performs the anointing in advance of his death.

Mark adds these words of Jesus: "She has done what she could" (Mark 14:8). That is also comforting for us! God does not ask of us what we cannot give. We cannot meet all the needs of the world, and God doesn't ask us to. Jesus' word about Mary brings peace to our hearts when too many demands are made upon us. It also helps us to overcome competitiveness and jealousy when we realize we cannot do what some others can do.

Jesus takes something which seems so insignificant outwardly and gives it a deeper meaning. When even a cup of cold water, given in Christ's name, is not overlooked, then we can be sure that unimpressive deeds of love have deep significance (Matt. 10:42).

Caring for the Poor

Jesus makes an important comment on the care of the needy. *You always have the poor with you* (John 12:8). That language is found in Deuteronomy 15:11, where Israel is exhorted to have an open hand for the needy, who will always be among them.

Jesus' words, however, must not be understood to mean that God has decreed that certain people should be wealthy and others poor. This heresy that a person's economic lot in life is divinely ordained was immortalized by Mrs. Alexander: "The rich man in his castle, the poor man at his gate. God made them high or lowly, and ordered their estate."

The early church understood Jesus' words to mean that it carried a constant obligation toward the poor. One can see this clearly from the opening pages of the book of Acts (2:45; 4:34; 6:1-7). The great missionary apostle, Paul, was constantly collecting monies for the poor (as in 1 Cor. 16:1-4). In the Decian persecution about the middle of the third century, the police broke into one of the churches in Rome, hoping to find money. When they asked the deacons where the treasures were, the deacons pointed to the hundreds of widows and orphans that were being fed daily by the church. "These are our treasures" was the answer.

Several years ago Senator Mark Hatfield of Oregon pleaded with Americans to reduce waste and live more frugally so that more could be done for the poor in the world. A reader of *Moodly Monthly* objected, "Our first charge from the Lord Jesus is to preach the gospel. There's no command to feed the world. According to God's Word, we will have the poor with us always." But that's not the language of the New Testament. The spread of the gospel and the ministry to the needy is all of one piece.

A Beautiful Thing

Jesus stresses the importance of good deeds. Mark informs us that Jesus tells Judas and the other disciples that Mary, by anointing him, has done a good deed, "a beautiful thing" (Mark 14:6, RSV). The word for *good* used here does not mean simply that which is morally good, but it has the meaning of service that is *beautiful, lovely, noble.* It's a goodness that strikes the eye.

Good deeds were much stressed in Judaism, and as time went on, there developed a kind of works righteousness. We cannot earn our way to heaven by good deeds, for we are saved by grace alone. However, as Paul explains in Ephesians 2:10, we have been saved "for good works."

Works are so important that John in one of his apocalyptic visions hears a beatitude pronounced on all those who die in the Lord "for their deeds follow them" (Rev. 14:13). Our good deeds go with us when we die. They are too important to be overlooked or lost or forgotten. Silver and gold will not go with us, but good deeds, the fruit of God's grace, become part of our lives. Indeed, John says "the righteous deeds of the saints" correspond to the wedding dress of the bride of Christ (the church), which she wears at the marriage supper of the Lamb (Rev. 19:7-8). Her dress is woven, as it were, out of deeds of love and mercy.

In Mark's Gospel Jesus assures Mary that her good deed will never be forgotten, for wherever the gospel will be preached in the world, this story will be told about Mary (Mark 14:9). And today, two thousand years later, we are still pondering the significance of what Mary did on that memorable occasion when she poured out the precious perfume on Jesus.

We are entering upon Passion Week and following our

Lord as he walks the ways of sorrows. Let us look for ways in which we can show him our love and our devotion. And let us remember the words of our Lord: "As you did it to one of the least of these who are members of my family, you did it to me" (Matt. 25:40).

7. Good Friday

The Richest Hill on Earth

They compelled a passer-by, who was coming in from the country, to carry his cross; it was Simon of Cyrene, the father of Alexander and Rufus. Then they brought Jesus to the place called Golgotha (which means the place of a skull). And they offered him wine mixed with myrrh; but he did not take it. And they crucified him, and divided his clothes among them, casting lots to decide what each should take.

It was nine o'clock in the morning when they crucified him. The inscription of the charge against him read, "The King of the Jews." And with him they crucified two bandits, one on his right and one on his left. Those who passed by derided him, shaking their heads and saying, "Aha! You who would destroy the temple and build it in three days, save yourself, and come down from the cross!" In the same way the chief priests, along with the scribes, were also mocking him among themselves and saying, "He saved others; he cannot save himself. Let the Messiah, the King of Israel, come down from the cross now, so that we may see and believe." Those who were crucified with him also taunted him.

(Mark 15:21-32)

Halford Luccock, one-time professor of preaching at

Yale, tells of an experience he had while driving through Montana. A friend was showing him the countryside, taking him through the valleys and hills between Helena and Butte. Suddenly his friend pointed to a mountain and exclaimed, "That's the richest hill on earth."

He was pointing to Silver Bow Mountain. From it silver and gold have been mined, and in the last century many billions of dollars worth of copper have been extracted.

But there is another hill, just outside Jerusalem which for altogether different reasons may be called the richest hill on earth. It is the hill called Calvary—a word derived from a Latin word meaning *skull;* its Semitic form is Golgotha. Perhaps it got this name because the hill looked like a skull, or because it was a place of death—but no one really knows.

Yet from this unimpressive hillock has come the greatest wealth the world has ever known. From Calvary's mountain has come the deliverance from evil powers, forgiveness of sins, the restoration of broken lives, the hope of eternal life. Calvary has inspired people throughout the centuries to make the greatest sacrifices, to produce the finest literature, to write the most powerful and moving hymnody.

It was at Calvary that God stepped into our human life with all its pains and misery and sin. Here on Calvary we who were once far away from God were reconciled and made members of the people of God (Eph. 2:12-14). And today we join with millions of Christ's followers all over the world to confess that Calvary is indeed the richest hill on earth.

Come with me, then, to this hill outside Jerusalem's city wall and witness the death of our Lord and Savior, Jesus Christ, through whom we have received life and peace. We want to do this by following Mark in his account of the sufferings of our Lord—an account that would never have been written were it not for Easter, when Christ broke the bonds of death and came forth triumphantly from the grave.

The Road to Calvary (Mark 15:21)

When I was a boy, living in southern Alberta, our Sunday school teacher taught us the children's song: "All the way to Calvary he went for me." Since we had all come to Canada only recently and did not yet know much English, neither the teacher nor we knew the meaning of the word *Calvary*. The teacher suggested, then, that we sing: "All the way to Calgary, he went for me." We had a sneaking suspicion that this bordered on sacrilege, but we joined in and sang our hearts out.

But now to our passage in Mark! A detachment of soldiers took Jesus and two other criminals through the busy streets of Jerusalem. It was custom that a soldier headed the procession and carried a plaque on which the crime of the condemned victim was written. Those condemned to crucifixion often had to carry the crossbeams on their shoulders.

Christian legend has it that Jesus' cross was made of the tree that stood in Paradise, the forbidden tree. From it, Adam and Eve had eaten, and that led to their expulsion from the garden of Eden. That's pure fancy, of course, and yet the story enshrines a sacred truth: Jesus, the last Adam, died because of the disobedience of the first Adam—a sin by which the latter dragged all of humanity into our present dilemma (Rom. 5:12-17; 1 Cor. 15:45).

After an exhausting night during which Jesus endured unspeakable tortures and insults, it was obvious that he would not be able to carry his crossbeam to Golgotha. The Roman centurion in charge must have feared that Jesus would die before he got to the place of crucifixion. Thus he impressed into service a man by the name of Simon.

To do this, a tap on the shoulder by a Roman soldier's spear was all that was required in a country occupied by the ruling power. No doubt Simon was an African Jew who had come from Cyrene to Jerusalem for the Passover. However, there were Cyrenian Jews who settled in Jerusalem and had their own synagogue (Acts 6:9).

Mark reports that Simon was coming in from the country when they forced him to carry the cross for Jesus. That doesn't mean that he had been working in the field, for this was not done at such holy seasons as Passover.

One can only imagine how Simon must have felt, both toward the Roman overlords who forced him into such a shameful act and toward Jesus who was the occasion of it all. How embarrassed he must have been to carry a criminal's cross in the eyes of the Jerusalem crowds!

I wish we knew more about Simon of Cyrene, but the Gospel writers are not simply historians or biographers; they are evangelists who want to proclaim the good news of Jesus' death, and so they omit many of the details of the road to the cross. But we do know that he was the father of Alexander and Rufus. Since Mark mentions their names, they may have been well known to the readers.

Could it be that this event in the life of their father was the beginning of their knowledge of the Savior? Did Jesus speak to Simon? Did Simon and his sons become followers of Jesus? We do not know, but this is a good guess since their names are given. In 1941 archaeologists digging on the slope of the Kidron Valley found a burial cave of Cyrenian Jews and an ossuary (a container with human remains) with the inscription "Alexander, son of Simon." Could this have been Simon's family grave? An intriguing question!

Mark sums up the way of sorrows that led our Lord to Calvary in one brief sentence: They brought Jesus to the place called Golgotha (Mark 15:22). Luke gives us a fuller account and reports some of the things Jesus said as he was led to the cross.

In Roman Catholic tradition there are fourteen stations on the way to the cross. The Gospels are largely silent on this point but the thought of reliving the way to Calvary has always had an important place in Christian devotion. The hymn writer sings, "Lest I forget Gethsemane, Lest I forget Thine agony; Lest I forget Thy love for me, *lead me to Calvary.*"

The Place Called Calvary (Mark 15:22-23)

They brought Jesus to the place called Golgotha. The verb *to bring* suggests that Jesus had to be helped along, perhaps carried, the final stretch of the way. But finally they reached the top of the hill. John tells us that the place was near the city (John 19:20). Executions were not to be carried out inside the city.

Early Christians made little of the place where Jesus was crucified. But in the fourth century Constantine had a basilica built at the spot where it was thought that our Lord had died. Throughout the centuries since then, Golgotha has attracted Christian pilgrims from many lands. This veneration of the place called Calvary can easily get out of bounds. When Christians begin to feel that prayers said on Calvary are more effective than those said elsewhere, they enter the realm of superstition. The early church made nothing of the place; it was far too interested in the meaning of Christ's death to pay much attention to the place.

When our Lord reached the hill called Golgotha, he must have been totally exhausted. So they offered him wine mingled with myrrh, but he didn't take it. According to an old tradition, respected women of Jerusalem provided a narcotic drink for those condemned to death in order to alleviate the pain. This humane practice was begun in response to the biblical injunction found in Proverbs

31:6–7, "Give strong drink to one who is perishing, and wine to those in bitter distress; let them drink and forget their poverty, and remember their misery no more." Possibly women offered this painkilling drink to Jesus (Mark has the indefinite *they* in 15:23).

But Jesus refused to drink it. Evidently he wanted to suffer the agony of the cross with full consciousness; he did not want his faculties to be numbed by this drug. After our Lord had tasted the agony of feeling forsaken by God because of our sins, he did accept the drink offered to him by one of the bystanders (Mark 15:36).

Mark has taken us with him to the place called Golgotha. He knows that his Greek readers won't understand that word, and so he translates it for them. He says it means *skull*. Those of you who have been to Israel have no doubt been shown a hill that looks a bit like a skull, with two holes on one side of the hill representing the eyesockets. But it is not at all certain that the appearance of the hill gave it the name *skull*.

Some think it was given this dreadful name because of the many skulls lying about, from former executions. Later Christian legend went so far as to suggest that it was the place where Adam's skull lay buried. That is pure imagination—but it's an attempt to bring the death of the last Adam, Jesus, into connection with the sin of the first Adam. As by one man's disobedience all of humankind was led into death, so by one man's obedience all of humanity is offered the gift of eternal life (Rom. 5:12-17).

Having then taken note of the road to Calvary, and the place called Calvary, let us now take a closer look at the cross of Calvary.

The Cross of Calvary (Mark 15:24-26)

The Crucifixion of Jesus

The Gospel writers all report this gruesome episode,

but they do so in the briefest manner possible. Mark sums it up in four words: *And they crucified him* (Mark 15:24). Why should he say more? The readers of that day knew only too well how brutal was this method of putting people to death.

Crucifixion evidently came into Mediterranean world from the Orient. It was now a Roman method of punishment, inflicted primarily on rebels of the lower classes—slaves, violent criminals, and the unruly elements in rebellious provinces, such as Judea. No Roman citizen was to be crucified.

In the unrest that followed the death of Herod the Great in 4 B.C., the Roman general, Varus, had no fewer than two thousand Galileans crucified. It was the height of brutality and humiliation. What added to the shame was that the victims were seldom buried, but were left exposed to wild beasts and the birds of prey.

When Paul later spoke of the scandal of the cross, or when he observed that the message of the cross was foolishness to the Greeks, he was not speaking in riddles. He was expressing a conviction born out of years of missionary preaching. Today the cross is worn as jewelry, but in the first century it was an obscenity. Cicero wrote (ca. 63 B.C.), "Let the very name of the cross be banished from the body and life of Roman citizens, and from their thoughts, eyes, and ears."

The story is told of a boy who saw a picture of the crucified Jesus hanging on the cross. It hurt his feelings—the cruel nails, the unfeeling spear. After looking at it for a long time, he turned away with the comment: "If God had been there, he would not have let them do it."

But God was there! "For God so loved the world that he gave his only Son" (John 3:16). God "did not withhold his own Son, but gave him up for all of us" (Rom. 8:32), "so that by the grace of God he might taste death for everyone" (Heb. 2:9).

One writer compares the cross to a freshly felled tree. One can see the rings of the tree where the saw cut through the log, but those rings run right up the trunk of the tree, even though we can't see them. So the cross, he says, is the visible appearance in this world of that love of God which stretches beyond our vision into the depths of eternity. For God "chose us in Christ before the foundation of the world" (Eph. 1:4).

We do not know precisely what kind of cross Jesus was crucified on. Likely the upright stakes were already standing on Calvary when Jesus and the two criminals arrived there. The victims were then bound or, as in the case of Jesus, nailed to the crossbeam on the ground. This crossbeam was then hoisted up and fastened to the upright stake. A Latin cross is one in which the crossbeam intersects the upright pole. One that looks like our capital T was later known as St. Anthony's cross. One in the form of an X came to be called St. Andrew's cross.

Normally the crosses were just high enough to raise the victim from the ground, and dogs and other beasts would tear at their flesh. If the victim was to be made clearly visible to the populace, that one was lifted onto a higher stake. And since a javelin or reed was later used to give Jesus the sponge filled with vinegar, his cross must have been fairly high, to underscore the grossness of his crime.

The cross became central in early Christian preaching. What some early believers found hard to understand is that the cross was not mentioned in the Old Testament—the Bible of the early church. But crucifixion was not a method of punishment in ancient Israel, where criminals were put to death by stoning. In the case of particularly heinous crimes, the victim was impaled on a stake after he was killed, and he was viewed as being under a divine curse.

Paul alludes to that understanding several times. He

quoted from Deuteronomy that everyone who hangs upon a tree is accursed (Deut. 21:23; a common execution then: see concordance). However, in the case of Jesus, we confess that he had borne God's curse not for his own sin but for our sin (Gal. 3:13; 2 Cor. 5:21).

The clothes of the crucified normally went to the executioners. We are informed that the soldiers divided Jesus' garments into four parts (John 19:23). The outer garment of Jesus was without a seam, and cutting it into four would have ruined it, and so they cast lots to see who would get it. That brought the words of the psalmist to John's mind, "They divided my clothes among themselves, and for my clothing they cast lots" (Ps. 22:18; John 19:24).

The Inscription Over the Crucified

As mentioned earlier, it was custom for the criminal or someone else to carry a board with words specifying the crime of the victim. In the case of Jesus, he was charged with being *THE KING OF THE JEWS* (Mark 15:26). This meant that he had been sentenced to death as a politically subversive rebel. That was the Roman explanation. For the Jews, this was an insult to have someone on a cross labeled as their king! They asked Pilate to have it changed to read: "This man said, I am King of the Jews." But Pilate by then was in a bad mood and refused to alter it (John 19:21-22).

This charge against Jesus was written in three languages: Latin, the language of government; Greek, the language of the world; and Hebrew (Aramaic), the language of Palestine. In a sense this was symbolic, for the whole world was somehow involved in the crucifixion. Moreover, the death of Christ has cosmic significance, for Christ is "the Lamb of God who takes away the sin of the world" (John 1:29).

In the eyes of the Romans, someone who claimed to be the king of the Jews was to be slapped down as a threat to

Caesar and the Roman power. In Jewish society, a claim to be king, Christ, or Messiah was explosive and would attract attention because of the many messianic expectations of the people and their yearning to be free from Roman oppression (Mark 13:22; John 6:15; Acts 5:36-37). Thus, to maintain the current compromises with the Romans, it was "expedient" for the temple leadership that a messianic pretender die. That was better than to arouse the wrath of the Romans to destroy the whole Jewish nation (John 11:50-51, KJV).

According to Richard Gardner, what really brought down the high priest's charge of blasphemy against Jesus was his claim to authority. Jesus told the high priest that "the one you are judging now will meet you later as your exalted judge from heaven!"[1] As Son of Man, he would be ruling the world from God's right hand, as God's prime minister (Mark 14:61-64).

In retrospect, that plaque on the cross of Jesus proclaims not just to the Jews but to all the world that Jesus is indeed king; he reigns from the tree. By his death he wins the lordship over the lives of men and women of every nation. By dying he triumphs over all evil powers. The kingdoms of this world are established by brute force, but the kingdom of God which endures forever is established by dying love.

"When I am lifted up from the earth," said Jesus, "[I] . . . will draw all people to myself" (John 12:32). This "lifting up" refers in the first instance to the cross. And as the one who was lifted up from the earth and nailed to the cruel tree on the first Good Friday, he draws men and women to himself even today. That's how his kingdom is established, his reign extended. "The head that once was crowned with thorns, Is crowned with glory now; A royal diadem adorns, the mighty Victor's brow."

The Mockery of the Crucified (Mark 15:27-32)

As our Lord hung upon the tree, people heaped insults on him. First of all, his companions in suffering mocked him. *And with him they crucified two bandits, one on his right and one on his left* (Mark 15:27). Luke informs us that one of them repented, but Mark simply says, *Those who were crucified with him also taunted him* (Mark 15:32). They were probably Zealots who may have taken part in the rebellion in which Barabbas participated (Mark 15:7-11). It has often been suggested that had Jesus not been condemned, Barabbas would have hung on his cross that day. Our Lord took the place of Barabbas. *And you and I are Barabbas!*

The fact that Jesus died in the company of evildoers reminded a later copyist of the Gospel of Mark of a passage in Isaiah 53:12, "He was counted among the lawless," and he inserted that prophetic word at this point (Mark 15:28). This quotation from Isaiah is found in Luke 22:37 but is omitted in the better manuscripts of Mark.

Not only the two thieves on the cross mocked Jesus, but also those who happened to pass by (Mark 15:29). They wagged their heads in derision. The chief priests and the scribes joined with them in the mockery. They say: *He saved others; he cannot save himself* (Mark 15:31). What they did not realize is that it was precisely because he did not save himself that he now can save others. He could have easily saved himself. He claimed to Peter in the hearing of those arresting him that he could call on legions of angels to deliver him if need be (Matt. 26:53). In the end, God did save him, when he raised him from the dead and delivered him from the powers of Hades.

But because Jesus was willing to lose his life, he now saves others, not only from physical death but also from eternal death. And that remains a permanent principle in the kingdom of God. Saving ourselves leads to loss, to poverty of soul, to emptiness; saving others leads to fullness of life. A grain of wheat that falls into the ground and dies, said Jesus, bears much fruit; but if it remains alone, it yields no harvest (John 12:24).

The story is told of the Christian sadhu, Sundhar Singh, that he was walking along a mountain pass with a companion one day. It became bitterly cold in the Himalayas, and a fierce snowstorm threatened their lives. Suddenly they came upon the body of a man who was nearly frozen to death. Singh's companion urged him to hurry or else they too would freeze. But Singh began to carry the dying man on his back, and thereby both men regained new warmth.

Singh's companion had hurried on by himself to save his life. Suddenly they came upon his body in the snow. He was frozen to death. Singh's willingness to lose his own life had saved it; the other man wanted to save his life and lost it.

The religious leaders watched Jesus dying. They called on him, the Messiah, the King of Israel, to come down from the cross, and then they will see and believe (Mark 15:32). Those words were spoken insincerely, but they express the attitude of many an unbeliever even today. They want to see and then they will believe. But that's the wrong order.

Jesus said to Martha, when her brother had died, that if she would believe, then she would see the glory of God (John 11:40). To doubting Thomas, the risen Lord said, "Blessed are those who have not seen and yet have come to believe." Did people believe on Jesus when they saw his many miracles? Did the Jewish leaders believe when Jesus raised Lazarus from the dead? No! "It's hard to believe," writes Dietrich Bonhoeffer, "because it's so hard to obey." It is when we believe, when we believe the gospel, when we put our trust in Christ, that it all begins to make sense, that we begin to see.

As we look at the richest hill on earth, I invite you also to put your faith in Jesus. You can trust the man who died for you. He will forgive all your sin, cover your past, give you a new life. He will make this day on which we remember his death a *good* Friday for you. Come to Calvary; it is indeed the richest hill on earth.

8. Easter

The Gospel of the Resurrection

Now I would remind you, brothers and sisters, of the good news that I proclaimed to you, which you in turn received, in which also you stand, through which also you are being saved, if you hold firmly to the message that I proclaimed to you—unless you have come to believe in vain.

For I handed on to you as of first importance what I in turn had received: that Christ died for our sins in accordance with the scriptures, and that he was buried, and that he was raised on the third day in accordance with the scriptures, and that he appeared to Cephas, then to the twelve. Then he appeared to more than five hundred brothers and sisters at one time, most of whom are still alive, though some have died. Then he appeared to James, then to all the apostles. Last of all, as to one untimely born, he appeared also to me. For I am the least of the apostles, unfit to be called an apostle, because I persecuted the church of God. But by the grace of God I am what I am, and his grace toward me has not been in vain. On the contrary, I worked harder than any of them—though it was not I, but the grace of God that is with me. Whether then it was I or they, so we proclaim and so you have come to believe. (1 Cor. 15:1-11)

I . . . remind you of the gospel (1 Cor. 15:1, NIV). That's the opening line of this great chapter on the resurrection. Had the Corinthians not heard the gospel? Had they not understood it? Of course they had. Paul had spent many months in Corinth proclaiming and explaining the good news of Jesus Christ.

But the readers needed to be reminded once again of the ABCs of the Christian message. Although the apostles encourage believers to be done with childish things and move on to greater maturity, the fundamental truths of the gospel need to be rehearsed again and again. The gospel is so unspeakably rich, it can be proclaimed in an infinite variety of ways.

The church lives not by its history (important though that is), but by the gospel. The spiritual life of the church does not depend on church buildings, but on the gospel. A church may be organized or structured to make it more effective, yet the church does not live by its structures, but by the gospel. It is in the gospel that the wells of salvation are opened up to us. The gospel shows us how to live in the darkness of this world. It is the gospel that sustains us in our trials and in our labors for the Lord. By the gospel the life of the church is constantly renewed.

The word *gospel* was originally not a biblical word. The Greek word *euangelion* means simply *good news.* The biblical writers picked up this word and filled it with new meaning. In the New Testament it is the good news of Christ's birth, of the coming of his kingdom. It is the good news of deliverance from death and sin and fear, the good news that God loves us in spite of our sin and fallenness, and that he has come to us in Jesus Christ in his mercy and grace.

Paul seems to have a special liking for the word *gospel;* the noun alone occurs some fifty-four times in his letters. It seems as if he can hardly write a paragraph without making reference to the gospel and to his call to be a messenger of the good news. Somehow the apostle could never get over it that God should have chosen him to be the bearer of the good news of redemption to the nations. "Of this gospel," he writes, "I have become a servant according to the gift of God's grace that was given me . . . the very least of all the saints . . . to bring to the Gentiles the news of the boundless riches of Christ" (Eph. 3:7-8).

At the very heart of the gospel is the good news that Christ rose from the dead. Today on Easter Sunday, we want to think together about the gospel of the resurrection.

The Rich Contents of the Gospel (1 Cor. 15:3-4)

Paul is careful to say that he did not dream up the gospel. He *received* it. And what he had received, he had passed on to the Corinthians. Our Gospels had not yet been written when Paul founded the church at Corinth. For an entire generation the good news was proclaimed orally before finished Gospel accounts were available (Luke 1:1-2). The great events of salvation lie at the very center of the good news: the death, the burial, and the resurrection of our Lord.

Do notice that these are all historical events. This makes the Christian faith so unique. Christianity is not simply a system of thought, a theology, a philosophy. The gospel is anchored in historical events which cannot be repeated—events which changed the history of the world; events which effect the ultimate destiny of humankind.

By contrast, Buddhism is a system of beliefs, based on the teachings of its founder, the Gautama. If Buddhism were wiped off the map, theoretically speaking, it could begin once again if someone should happen to have the same ideas and begin to propagate them. But Christianity is rooted in events that took place in Bethlehem, in Galilee, and outside the walls of Jerusalem two thousand years ago, when the Son of God was crucified and then rose triumphantly from the dead. Note well, then, the basic ingredients of the gospel as found in the opening verses of this chapter!

The Death of Christ

That Christ died for our sins in accordance with the scriptures (1 Cor. 15:3). But how can the death of an innocent person be good news? Death is a tragedy. Death is never viewed as a friend in the Bible. Death is the last enemy that needs to be overcome. And the fact that Jesus was condemned by a Roman judge could only mean that Jesus had died as a criminal. And that's not good news!

How then can Paul speak of Christ's shameful death as good news? The answer lies in a little preposition. He died *for* our sins. He didn't die as a criminal. He wasn't condemned to death because he had violated the laws of the land. He wasn't under the curse of God. He died on our behalf. His was a death for others. He took our place.

In Rembrandt's painting *The Three Crosses* the artist pictures the crowd around the crosses witnessing the awful tragedy of Christ's death. At the edge of the painting there is another figure, almost hidden in the shadows. Art critics tell us that is a representation of Rembrandt himself. It was his way of saying, "My sins helped to nail him there." *He died for our sins.*

And all this happened, says Paul, *in accordance with the scriptures.* But where does the Old Testament speak of Christ's death? Jewish readers thought the sufferings of the servant of God in Isaiah 53 were those of Israel. Christians, however, read the Old Testament from the vantage point of the cross and the resurrection and see in Isaiah 53 a clear further reference to the death of Christ. To say that he died according to the Scriptures was a way of saying that his death was in the plan of God; it was no accident. Christ is "the Lamb slain from the foundation of the world" (Rev. 13:8, KJV).

The Burial of Jesus

And that he was buried (1 Cor. 15:4). All four Gospels tell the story of Christ's burial. Joseph of Arimathea provided the garden tomb. Criminals were often left unburied—their bodies thrown to the beasts and the vultures. It was always considered an act of piety when people gave the dead a proper burial. Jesus' friends buried him. He had not simply fainted or lost consciousness. He was dead; and burial confirms that. In his Pentecost sermon Peter said that David "both died and was buried, and his tomb is with us to this day" (Acts 2:29). There's something awfully final about burial.

Although Paul does not explicitly say that his burial also was in accordance with the Scriptures, I think it must be assumed. Our minds go back once more to Isaiah 53:9, "They made his grave with the wicked and his tomb with the rich."

In his sermon at Antioch of Pisidia, Paul recalls that "they took him down from the tree and laid him in a tomb": they buried him. But that was not the end of the story. "God raised him from the dead" (Acts 13:29-30). Thus the burial was but the prelude to the resurrection. And that is the third item Paul mentions as constituting the core of the gospel.

The Resurrection of Jesus

He was raised on the third day in accordance with the scriptures (1 Cor. 15:4). Is there a reference to Christ's resurrection in the Scriptures? Peter quotes Psalm 16:10 in his Pentecost sermon: "For you will not abandon my soul to Hades, or let your Holy One experience corruption" (Acts

2:27). Whether Paul also had such passages in mind is not clear. There is a passage in Hosea 6:2 that speaks of the third day: "After two days he will revive us; on the third day he will raise us up, that we may live before him." This passage originally referred to the spiritual renewal of Israel but was later understood also as a reference to the resurrection.

We do not know precisely which Scriptures Paul had in mind, but he saw the entire Old Testament as a preparation for this climactic event of salvation history—the resurrection of Jesus. For the early Christians, Jesus' resurrection was so important that they began to worship on the first day of the week (1 Cor. 16:2). They called this day *the Lord's day* (Rev. 1:10), for on the first Easter Sunday Christ had arisen as Lord over death and hell. Even Jewish Christians, for whom the Sabbath had been the heart of their Jewish faith, came together on the first day of the week to confess Jesus as Lord. And when Christians gathered for meals at which they remembered the Lord's death, they called it the *Lord's Supper* (1 Cor. 11:20).

Had it not been for the resurrection, many of the sayings of Jesus would not have been remembered; his mighty deeds of power might have been left unrecorded. For if he had stayed in the tomb, he would have shown himself to be an impostor. His shameful death would have been unmitigated tragedy.

If Christ had not been raised from the dead, says Paul, we would still be in our sins, all those who died would be lost, and we ourselves would be of all people most to be pitied (1 Cor. 15:13-19).

A. M. Hunter of Aberdeen once wrote a book *The Work and Words of Jesus,* in which the last chapter deals with the resurrection of Jesus. The Queen Mother came upon the book and read it and then wrote to Hunter: "I am sorry to say that I read the last chapter first, which is, I know, dreadful cheating; but it makes a wonderful and hopeful background for the rest of the book, and I do not regret it at all."

Yes, indeed, the resurrection of our Lord is the first and the last and the dominating element in the New Testament. What happened at Easter overwhelmed Christ's followers to such an extent that it dominated their thinking and became the very heart and center of their preaching.

Elton Trueblood, a Quaker philosopher and the author of scores of books, was a skeptic in the earlier years of his life. The resurrection was one truth he could not accept. However, he was slowly convinced of the reality of the resurrection as he studied the life of the early church. He writes: "In a short time these broken men became strong, confident, and bold as lions. They sang; they rejoiced; they healed; they taught; they suffered triumphantly. And this they did not only for a few days of passing enthusiasm, but for the remainder of their lives." That convinced him of the reality of the resurrection.

Paul writes: "If you confess with your lips that Jesus is Lord and believe in your heart that God raised him from the dead, you will be saved" (Rom. 10:9).

These are foundation truths of the gospel which give the good news such a rich content—passed on to us through many witnesses.

Many Witnesses to the Gospel (1 Cor. 15:5-11)

The Early Witnesses

And that he appeared to Cephas [Peter] (1 Cor. 15:5). On the first Easter morning, our Lord appeared to a group of faithful women who had come to the tomb where Jesus lay buried. They were frightened to death by the sight of the heavenly messenger, who spoke to calm their fears and send them to tell his disciples that Jesus had been raised from the dead. Then he added, "And [tell] Peter" (Mark

16:6-7). And when the Emmaus disciples returned to Jerusalem, they reported: "The Lord has risen indeed, and he has appeared to Simon!" (Luke 24:34).

The apostles draw a veil over that meeting with Peter. We can only surmise what must have transpired. Peter, the leader of the apostolic band, had promised that he would rather die than deny his Lord. But he had failed and had wept his eyes out. And now the risen Lord appears to Peter. There are times when we too feel we have failed and disappointed our Lord; we are disgusted with ourselves, ashamed, and broken. And to such failures, the risen Christ comes even today and offers forgiveness and hope.

Then to the twelve (1 Cor. 15:5). Judas was no longer with the apostles, but *the twelve* persists as a technical term for the founders of the church. If the reference here is to the first Easter Sunday, then Thomas was not with them either, so that in fact only ten apostles were gathered. But they are still called *the twelve*.

After the crucifixion and burial of Jesus, the twelve had hidden behind closed doors, trembling at every knock. But after the risen Christ appeared to them, they were transformed. Fear gave way to courage, doubt to certainty, disappointment to radiant faith. Soon they were out on the streets with the good news of the resurrection, announcing that Jesus was now Lord over all.

This created a great stir and brought the wrath of the unbelieving Jews down upon their heads. Peter and John were imprisoned; James was beheaded with the sword; and if we are to trust some of the later traditions, most of the twelve suffered because of their witness to the risen Christ—some to the point of death.

Then he appeared to more than five hundred brothers and sisters at one time, most of whom are still alive, though some have died (1 Cor. 15:6). This is the only reference in the New Testament to the appearance of the risen Christ to five hundred of his followers. Although some of these had died by the time Paul wrote his letter to the Corinthians, most of them were still alive. They could be called upon as witnesses to the reality of Christ's resurrection.

By mentioning Christ's appearance to the five hundred, Paul underscores that the reports of Jesus' resurrection were not lies or false rumors. We recall that the Jewish leaders had bribed the soldiers to spread the rumor that the disciples had stolen the body of Jesus and were now proclaiming that he had risen from the dead (Matt. 28:11-15). Paul rings down the curtain on such nonsense. When Paul wrote this letter, there were still hundreds of people around who had seen the risen Christ with their own eyes. They could be asked. Among them was also a brother of our Lord, James.

Then he appeared to James (1 Cor. 15:7). The Gospels do not mention this event. Likely the brother of Jesus is meant. Jesus' brothers at first did not believe in him (John 7:5; Mark 3:31-35; 6:3). James, like the other brothers, had initially resisted the teachings of Jesus. When they put Jesus to death on Calvary, James must have been filled with remorse and yearned for a word of forgiveness from his brother. But Jesus was dead.

However, when the grave gave up its prey, our Lord made it a point of meeting his brother James, and he became a humble follower of Jesus. There is an apocryphal story that James had actually made a vow when Jesus was crucified that he would neither eat nor drink until his brother rose from the grave. And after the resurrection, Jesus sought him out. When they met, Jesus said: "Brother James, eat and drink, for the son of man is risen from the dead."[1]

In Galatians 2:9 James is paired with Peter as a leader of the Jerusalem church. Paul even calls him one of the pillars of the church in that chapter. James defended the cause of Christian Gentiles at the Jerusalem Conference (Acts 15:13-21), and it may well be that he is the author of the letter of James.

The Jewish historian, Josephus, reports that James was killed by Jewish leaders a few years before the destruction of Jerusalem in A.D. 70. According to Eusebius, some of the Jews surmised that Jerusalem suffered such a terrible fate because James was no longer praying for his people. Christian tradition tells us that he had calloused knees from praying so much for the salvation of his people.[2] No doubt the meeting of the risen Christ with his brother James was the secret of the powerful witness of this early leader of the Jerusalem church.

There were other witnesses to the resurrection, and what we have here is not exhaustive. The Gospels record other meetings. The list of witnesses in our text is given to take away all doubt on the part of the readers about the resurrection of Jesus. But Paul must mention one other witness. He too had seen the risen Christ.

A Later Witness
   Last of all, as to one untimely born, he appeared also to me (1 Cor. 15:8). There was a time in Paul's life when he viewed Christ as an enemy of all that he held dear and precious. So convinced was he that Jesus was a menace to the Jewish religion that he did the unusual: as a rabbi in the Pharisaic tradition, he turned into a fierce persecutor of Christians—something he had not learned from his teacher, Gamaliel. However, on his way to Damascus, the risen Christ met him, and all that he had counted gain turned into loss (Phil. 3:6-7). After his encounter with the living Lord, Paul became a flaming witness of the gospel.

   Because of his past, Paul always speaks about his calling to be a messenger of the good news with deep humility. He says he is really not worthy to be called an apostle, and attributes all that he is to the grace of God (1 Cor. 15:9-10). In his unbelief he had persecuted men and women who had confessed faith in Jesus. He had dragged them off to prison and death. He had even tried to get Christians to curse Jesus, but they chose death rather than denying their Lord (Acts 26:10-11).

But on the way to Damascus Christ had met Paul and stopped him in his mad endeavors. In a sense it was a violent encounter, so different from the meetings with the risen Christ which he has just been listing. Paul speaks of himself as one who was *born untimely* by using *ektrōma*, the Greek word for *miscarriage* or *abortion*. Other apostles had heard the call of Jesus and followed him; Paul came into the kingdom violently, as it were. And so he thinks of himself as *the least of the apostles* (1 Cor. 15:9). *The grace of God* is the only explanation he can give for the fact that he is now Christ's apostle (1 Cor. 15:10).

Humility has characterized true saints throughout the history of the Christian church. William Carey, the father of modern missions, wrote to John Rylands in England in 1823: "I have long made the language of Psalm 51 my own, 'Have mercy upon me, O God . . . according to the multitude of thy tender mercies blot out my transgressions.' Should you outlive me and have influence to prevent it, I earnestly request that no epithets of praise may ever accompany my name. All such expressions would convey a falsehood. To me belong shame and confusion of face. I can only say, 'Hangs my helpless soul on Thee' " (Charles Wesley). Carey, too, had seen that everything he had accomplished was by the grace of God.

To be humble doesn't mean self-denigration, however. And Paul goes on immediately to speak of his work in the kingdom of God. Latecomer though he was, he strove to make up for lost time. Without boasting, he can say that he worked harder than others. However, lest anyone should think he is boasting, he quickly adds, *Though it was not I, but the grace of God that is with me* (1 Cor. 15:10). One might think of God's grace as a companion who stood beside him and did the work.

Nevertheless, Paul did not stand idly by. He threw himself into the work of the kingdom with holy zeal and established centers of Christian light and hope in the lands surrounding the Aegean Sea. However, he does not want to be seen as a Lone Ranger. He preached basically the same gospel that other apostles proclaimed. But, *Whether then it was I or they, so we proclaim and so you have come to believe* (1 Cor. 15:11). And to this gospel the Corinthians had responded in faith.

Personal Response to the Gospel (1 Cor. 15:1-2)

Let us now go back to the beginning of our passage, which I purposely left to the last. Here is where the issues are joined; here we have to make a decision; here is where it becomes personal.

They Received the Gospel.

Now I would remind you, brothers and sisters, of the good news that I proclaimed to you, which you in turn received (1 Cor. 15:1). *Receiving* is another way of saying *believing.*

In one sense every Christian has *received* the gospel. No one creates or discovers the gospel on his or her own. The gospel goes back to Jesus. He is the source and origin of the good news. Paul had also received the gospel. and the Corinthians had received it from the apostle Paul. They had welcomed the good news, said Yes to the call of the gospel, embraced it by faith, staked their future on it, and were now seeking to order their lives by it.

They Stand in the Gospel.

The good news . . . in which also you stand (1 Cor. 15:1). The gospel gave the Corinthians ground under their feet. Their acceptance of the gospel was not a one-day novelty; they stood clinging firmly to the truths of the gospel; they walked in its light.

At the turn of the century a delegation from Berlin came to Tübingen, where the famous New Testament scholar Adolf Schlatter taught. They wanted to persuade him to come to Berlin. But before they took any further steps, they wanted to clarify one point: "Is it true," they asked, "that you stand *on* the Word of God?" They thought that was a bit old-fashioned. Schlatter promptly responded, "No, gentlemen, I stand *under* the word of God." There is a difference!

The Corinthians were standing in the gospel. However, verse 2 sounds a note of warning. It speaks of holding fast the gospel and even suggests that a person can believe in vain. "We have become partners of Christ," says the writer of the Hebrews, "if only we hold our first confidence firm to the end" (Heb. 3:14).

They Are Saved by the Gospel.

Through which also you are being saved (1 Cor. 15:2). It is worth noting the tense of the verb "saved." It speaks of continuing action: *You are being saved.* That's why Paul was "not ashamed of the gospel" because "it is the power of God for salvation to everyone who has faith" (Rom. 1:16).

There is a sense in which salvation is a once-for-all experience, and so it is quite appropriate to use the past tense: we "have been saved" (Eph. 2:5, 8). But salvation is also an ongoing experience. It even has a future dimension: we wait for him unto salvation—final deliverance (Rom. 13:11). This side of heaven we can never fully experience what Christ did for us when he delivered us from sin and death. We have the firstfruits of the Spirit (Rom. 8:23). But while we wait for the full harvest, we experience the powers of the age to come (Heb. 6:5). By the gospel we are being saved (cf. 1 Cor. 1:18; 2 Cor. 6:2; Phil. 2:12-13).

The question for us today: How do we respond to this gospel? Is there someone on this Easter Sunday, this resurrection day, who has not yet confessed Christ as Lord? And, I ask those of you who have received the gospel, do you *stand* in the gospel? Do you have a firm grip on it in the sense that you understand its essence? Have you embraced it with all your heart? Does it make any difference in your life?

O wonderful words of the gospel!
   O wonderful message they bring!
Proclaiming a blessed redemption,
   Through Jesus our Savior and King.

9. Low Sunday

An Encounter with the Risen Christ

Now on that same day two of them were going to a village called Emmaus, about seven miles from Jerusalem, and talking with each other about all these things that had happened. While they were talking and discussing, Jesus himself came near and went with them, but their eyes were kept from recognizing him. And he said to them, "What are you discussing with each other while you walk along?" They stood still, looking sad. Then one of them, whose name was Cleopas, answered him, "Are you the only stranger in Jerusalem who does not know the things that have taken place there in these days?" He asked them, "What things?" They replied, "The things about Jesus of Nazareth, who was a prophet mighty in deed and word before God and all the people, and how our chief priests and leaders handed him over to be condemned to death and crucified him. But we had hoped that he was the one to redeem Israel. Yes, and besides all this, it is now the third day since these things took place. Moreover, some women of our group astounded us. They were at the tomb early this morning, and when they did not find his body there, they came back and told us that they had indeed seen a vision of angels who said that he was alive. Some of those who were with us went to the tomb and found it just as the women had said; but they did not see him." Then he said to them, "Oh, how foolish you are, and how slow of heart to believe all that the prophets have declared! Was it not necessary that the Messiah should suffer these things and then enter into his glory?" Then beginning with Moses and all the prophets, he interpreted to them the things about himself in all the scriptures.

As they came near the village to which they were going, he walked ahead as if he were going on.   (Luke 24:13-28)

The Sunday after Easter has come to be known as *low* Sunday. The Lenten season reaches its high point with Easter. The celebration of Christ's glorious resurrection from the dead transports us, as it were, into another world. But the next day, the next week, we are back in the workaday world; we are faced with the problems of this world; we suffer from weariness, disappointments, and losses. This can cause feelings of depression.

No doubt we have all experienced such low points in our life. After some mountaintop experience, we had to walk through a deep valley. Perhaps for some of us this is a *low* Sunday. The story of the encounter of the Emmaus disciples with the risen Christ speaks to such a situation.

After his glorious resurrection from the dead, our Lord appeared to a number of individuals and groups of people both in Jerusalem and in Galilee. Our passage tells of two distraught followers of Jesus who were met by the risen Lord on the way to their home in Emmaus. It is one of those immortal short stories of the New Testament which rarely fails to move the reader. Malcolm Muggeridge, a man of great literacy skill who was converted to Christ in his old age, says of the Emmaus account: "The story is so incredibly vivid that I swear to you, no one who has tried to write, can doubt its authenticity. There is something in the very language and manner of it, which breathes truth."[1]

Let us enter into this account. It is late afternoon on the first Christian Easter. These two followers of Jesus, not mentioned elsewhere in the New Testament, wend their weary way to the little village of Emmaus, several miles northwest of Jerusalem. Its exact identity is still disputed.

With thousands of other Jews they have attended the Passover in Israel's mother city, Jerusalem, commemorating the great deliverance from Egypt. This event marked the beginning of Israel's national existence. But this year the festival has taken a strange turn. The prophet of Nazareth, to whom these two have given their allegiance, has fallen prey to the religious bigotry of the Jewish leaders. The light of the world has been snuffed out by human darkness; divine love has been overcome by human hatred; the one who promised his followers eternal life has been conquered by death. All their hopes lie shattered on the ground, like a dream that vanishes upon awakening.

To add to their confusion, rumor had it that the prophet of Nazareth has risen from the grave. They are puzzled and perplexed by the enigma and mystery of it all. What else is there to do but to turn their backs on the whole debacle and go home! With heavy step they trudge along, the evening sun blinding their eyes. Suddenly a stranger joins them. Their senses are still numb from the tragedy they have witnessed in the past few days, and so they see nothing unusual about this unknown companion.

Luke explains that their eyes are held from recognizing him. God in his mysterious wisdom evidently blocks their inner sight because he wants to give them a vision of the risen Lord, such as they will never forget as long as they live. This encounter with the risen Christ is to turn their sunset into a glad morning, their feelings of heaviness into shouts of joy. And that's so typical of the Christian way.

On the psychological level, things don't remain on an even keel. We suffer blows to our inner life, our feelings are hurt, we suffer disappointment, we are depressed, and we need to be lifted up again. And that is true also on the spiritual plane. Sometimes faith seems to be at full tide: God is near, his blessings are patently obvious. Then there are those times of emptiness when we are in the trough of the waves.

The story of the Emmaus disciples speaks to all those who may be in the slough of despondency. It lifts us up and puts heart into us. It's the kind of story that can help us face tomorrow. The Christ who appears to these disappointed disciples is alive, and he wants to meet us in our needs on the way to our Emmaus.

Obstacles to Encountering the Risen Christ

The Mood of Gloom

They stood still, looking sad (Luke 24:17). They are distraught; deep melancholy has settled over their lives. They have suffered an unspeakable loss; the one on whom they had pinned their hopes for a new and better day had been shamefully put to death. On that black Friday when Jesus was crucified, the bottom had dropped out of their life.

We had hoped that he was the one to redeem Israel, they complain (Luke 24:21). Had they been duped? Had an impostor uttered such words of grace and done such mighty deeds? There are so many messianic pretenders in the land. Has Jesus been just one of their kind?

Their eyes are, one might say, so full of tears that they fail to see that the risen Christ is walking with them. And that's true of our life also. Robert Robinson, the seventeenth-century author of the beautiful hymn, "Come Thou Fount of Every Blessing," was traveling on a stagecoach while deeply depressed. Beside him sat a lady who was reading a book. Suddenly she came across several lines of a hymn that seemed so overwhelmingly beautiful that she called them to the attention of Robinson, who was otherwise a stranger to her. He tried to lead the conversation in a different direction, but she wanted him to see these wonderful lines. Finally he said, "Lady, I am that unhappy man who wrote the words of that hymn many years ago, and I would give a thousand worlds if I could again enjoy the feelings I had then."

All of us, I think, can identify with that story. It happens to the greatest saints. In the Middle Ages the monks spoke of a disease they called *sicitas,* dryness, which was particularly bad on Mondays. On Sundays they would often exhaust themselves emotionally in spiritual exercises and then feel like a flat tire the day after.

Perhaps you are weighed down with a heavy spirit. That does not necessarily mean that you have committed some great evil or that your faith has been shattered. But it could be that you have had some loss, some disappointment, some failure, some tragedy, some bad news. And that makes it hard for you to see the risen Christ, who is walking with you on the way.

Unresolved Questions

As they talked and discussed, Jesus himself drew near and . . . said to them, "What are you talking about to each other, as you walk along?" (Luke 24:15, 17, GNB). Questions are legitimate. We learn by asking questions. When the little ones ask the same questions over and over again, we tire of them. But it's sad when we stop asking questions.

Some of the great saints of the Bible had serious questions about God's ways, and sometimes they hurled them at God in their distress. Moses implored the Lord God not to destroy the Israelites after they had worshiped the golden calf. If the Lord wouldn't forgive his people, Moses asked to have his own name blotted out of the book of the righteous (Exod. 32). Then Job couldn't understand why God would let him, an innocent person, suffer. Somehow he felt God owed him an answer (Job 26—31).

Think of the psalmist Asaph, who could not understand why the godless seemed to have a better life than he who washed his hands in innocence (Ps. 73). Or take that devout skeptic, Habakkuk, who was perplexed by God's government of the world. He couldn't see why a holy God could allow the godless Babylonians overwhelm the land of Judah (Hab. 1).

Often our life too is like a picture puzzle in which a few pieces are missing. But we don't throw out the puzzle immediately, for we still hope that the missing pieces will turn up some day, and then the picture will be complete.

However, it is possible to become so caught up in unanswered questions that we lose hold of God and lose the joy of walking the Christian way. God's Word gives us the answers to the basic questions of this life and the life to come —enough light for the way. But many questions will have to wait for an answer when Christ calls us to himself and all the enigmas of life are cleared up. So let us not be overwhelmed by unanswered questions. In God's own time the answers will be given.

Lack of Understanding

Oh, how foolish you are, and how slow of heart to believe all that the prophets have declared! (Luke 24:25). Those are hard words. The two on the Emmaus road are asking questions, but from a limited perspective. Their understanding of God's plan of redemption, their hope of messianic salvation, is too narrow. They have not understood that the redemption which Jesus came to bring was not narrowly nationalistic.

Jesus aimed to restore Israel as a people open to be joined by any believers, not to recover the military greatness of David's rule. He did not come to overthrow the Roman tyranny. His kingdom was not from this world, and that's why his followers wouldn't fight, as he explained to

Pilate (John 19:36). Rather, Jesus came to gather a new people of God, to establish God's reign over the hearts and lives of all those who acknowledge him as king, and to rule over the whole world (Luke 6:12-16; 9:1-6; 22:69; 24:26).

No doubt the Emmaus disciples have some knowledge of the prophets, but they have not understood *all* the prophets, as Jesus pointed out (Luke 24:25). Perhaps they have picked out only that strand of prophetic teaching that speaks of Davidic kingship and have overlooked what the prophet Isaiah said about the suffering servant. In any case, their confusion and sorrow come at least in measure from their lack of understanding.

And is it not true that some of our own sorrows are caused by lack of understanding, by lack of perspective? Paul wrote to the Thessalonians about those of their members who had died: "We do not want you to be uninformed, brothers and sisters, about those who have died, so that you may not grieve as others do who have no hope" (1 Thess. 4:13). To overcome their sorrow, they needed insight to strengthen their hope.

Once the Emmaus disciples see that the kingdom of God is to be established through suffering and death, that the cross is on the way to glory, the clouds are driven from their lives. In a similar manner new rays of light from God's Word can make all the difference in our lives.

Here then are several obstacles that stand in the way of an encounter with the risen Christ: The mood of gloom, unresolved questions, and minds that fail to understand God's plans.

Conditions for Encountering the Risen Christ

Childlike Confidence

Although the Emmaus disciples are confused and disappointed, their high estimate of Jesus remains unshaken.

When Jesus joins them and prods them to share with him the subject of their conversation, they say, *Why, you mean to say you have not heard of Jesus of Nazareth, who was a prophet mighty in deed and word before God and all the people?* (based on Luke 24:18-19).

Their understanding of the way in which God would establish his kingdom is limited, but they can never free themselves from the deep impressions which Jesus made on them. They can not understand why their leaders acted so perversely and so cruelly, or why God allowed such a good and godly man to die so shamefully. But they have faith. They have placed their confidence in Jesus, and that they can not shake off.

At times in life we, too, run up against problems—problems in our Christian walk, in the life of faith, for which there are no easy answers. We may be tempted to throw our faith overboard. In the late forties I was a student at the University of British Columbia. A young man from our church was enrolled in a psychology course. In it he was confronted with numerous questions to which he could not find answers from the standpoint of his Christian faith. I suppose he wanted pat answers. In any case he was not willing to wait or to grapple with the issues, and so he rejected the Christian faith.

Jesus told Peter on one occasion, when this disciple was befuddled, "You do not know now what I am doing, but later you will understand" (John 13:7).

The Emmaus disciples had unanswered questions, to be sure, but they still had a childlike confidence in the one whom they had learned to love. Such confidence is often more important than to have answers to the many questions that life throws at us.

A Burning Heart
After they shared their grief with the unknown compan-

ion who joined them on the way, that stranger begins to explain the Scriptures to them. Beginning with Moses and all the prophets, he interprets for them *the things about himself* in sacred history (Luke 24:27). In retrospect they confess: "Were not our hearts burning within us while he was talking to us on the road, while he was opening the scriptures to us?" (Luke 24:32).

In Hebrew psychology, the heart is the fulcrum of life; that's where people think, where they make decisions, where they feel. What persons are in reality, they are in the heart, not on the face or on the lips. These Emmaus disciples are stirred to the very depths of their being as they listen to Christ's interpretation of the Scriptures. And as they listen with burning hearts, it suddenly all makes sense.

To have a burning heart has nothing to do with a warm sensation inside, and so I don't want anyone here to feel guilty if they do not feel any strong emotions rising up within them. It means rather to have a deep interest in the things of God. Spiritual indifference closes the door to an encounter with the risen Christ, but a burning heart is an invitation for him to meet us.

A lover of nature used to tell his friends about all the wonders of the woods—the secret habits of birds and bugs and beetles. Some of them became so interested that they tried to see these marvelous things, too, but came back disappointed. When they confessed that they hadn't seen very much, he explained: "You have to be willing to lie in a wet ditch for several hours."

I have never been excited about the debates concerning the nature of Christ, those controversies in the early centuries of the Christian church. But I am impressed with the enthusiasm people manifested. Gregory of Nyssa in the fourth century wrote: "If I ask for my bill, the reply is a comment on the virgin birth; if I ask for a piece of bread, I am told that the Father is greater than the Son; when I ask whether my bath is ready, I am told that the Son was created from nothing."

Much of that was hairsplitting, we would say. But to their eternal credit, it must be said that they wanted to be sure they correctly understood what the Scriptures said about the nature of Christ. A childlike confidence and a burning heart go a long way in providing the proper setting for an encounter with the risen Christ.

Christ Entering into Their Problems

The encounter with the risen Christ begins when Jesus draws near and walks with them. He asks respectfully: *What are those words you are throwing back and forth?* (Luke 24:17, DE). Very tactfully he wins their confidence. He does not force himself into their lives.

William Barclay tells of a minister who used to visit him upon occasion when he was a young man just beginning his pastoral calling. This visitor would say to him, "Well now Willie, let it all hang out." And Barclay says, "I always clammed up." Our Lord does not violate people's sensitivities. He simply makes himself available. He asks about their hurts and pains and disappointments. He listens to them. And although he is a stranger, they are willing to open up to him, and he enters their lives.

Much of the Psalm literature is an outpouring of the heart. We have laments, complaints, cries, petitions, praise, and thanksgiving. There are psalms in which no petitions are made; the psalmist simply describes his condition before God—his hurts and pain and fears and disappointments. And that's no doubt one reason why New Testament believers find it so easy to identify with the psalmists. They teach us how to pray.

The weary travelers to Emmaus pour out their grief, and the risen Lord, who enters into their lives, gives them the oil of joy for their mourning.

Christ Opening the Scriptures

We have already noted that much of the frustration of these disciples comes from the fact that they have not understood their Scriptures correctly. Our Lord then expounds Moses and the prophets for them, and that prepares for the realization that they are in the presence of the risen Christ.

We too can meet the risen Christ in the pages of God's Word. Yet it is possible to study the Scriptures and not have an encounter with Jesus. Jesus accused his contemporaries: "You search the scriptures because you think that in them you have eternal life. . . . Yet you refuse to come to me to have life" (John 5:39-40).

Sometimes we are not in the frame of mind to have an encounter with the risen Christ in his Word. John Bunyan writes in his autobiography, *Grace Abounding,* that he had times in his life when the Scriptures seemed to be dry as a stick to him. But then there were times when he was completely overwhelmed by the riches that flowed from them.

Christ meets us unexpectedly in the strangest places and circumstances. But I think you will agree that it is supremely in the pages of the Scriptures that Christ comes to us and speaks to us his words of comfort, correction, and healing.

Christ Opening Their Eyes

The opening of the Scriptures is but the prelude to the opening of their eyes. When they arrive at their home in Emmaus, these two disciples ask the stranger into their home. He has listened to their problems and so wondrously opened up the Scriptures to them. As they sit down at the table and Jesus breaks the bread, their eyes are opened and they recognize him.

They are like the poet who looked out of his window at night and could not see the moon or the stars. Then suddenly a gust of wind moved the branches and the leaves of the tree, and he saw the moon in all its brightness. He broke out in words, "Infinities hidden by a leaf, constellations hidden by a branch." His eyes were opened.

We need open eyes if we are to encounter the risen Christ in our daily lives. Sometimes we see him when we break bread together at communion; sometimes in the way he supplies our daily bread; sometimes in the stillness of the forest, the mountain, the field; sometimes in the midst of sorrow and pain; and sometimes in the dull routine of daily toil.

Some years ago a Gospel of Thomas was found in Egypt. It does not belong to our New Testament, but it purports to have in it sayings of Jesus not recorded in our canonical Gospels. One of his sayings goes like this: "Lift the stone and I am there; split the wood and you will find me."[2] The meaning seems to be that Christ can be found amid the toils of life, whether one is a stone mason or a carpenter. But we need open eyes to see Christ.

Blessings of Encountering the Risen Christ

New Courage

It is toward evening when the Emmaus disciples reach their home. They have walked some seven miles from Jerusalem. But after recognizing the Lord, they immediately turn around and walk back again (Luke 24:33).

We all know how enervating discouragement and disappointment can be physically. Conversely, renewed courage can greatly strengthen our bodies.

A moment ago they were begging Jesus to stay with them for it was almost evening. But now that doesn't seem to matter. They decide to return to Jerusalem and tell the disciples. They went to Emmaus to forget it all, but now with hearts healed and filled with new joy, they leave Emmaus and go back to Jerusalem. Things have turned

around. Now they know that there is grace beyond tragedy, there is hope beyond death, there is love beyond hatred.

Has that not been our experience, too? When it was
midnight in our souls, when we were battered with the
winds of adversity, when our minds were reeling with per-
plexity—then the risen Christ came to us. We saw him
with the eyes of faith, and our strength was renewed.

Their hearts were given back to them, and they could
not wait to tell others.

A Testimony

Arriving in Jerusalem at a late hour, they find the eleven
still awake, together, and sharing the overwhelming news
that the Christ who died, whom they forsook and denied,
is alive. And then the two disciples of Emmaus open up to
the eleven and tell the exciting story of how they encountered the risen Christ on the road (Luke 24:35).

William Sangster, great Methodist preacher of England,
lay dying in 1960. It was Easter morning. He had already
lost his voice and could no longer speak. So he wrote a
note to his daughter: "How terrible to wake up on an Easter morning without a voice with which to shout, 'He is ris-
en.' But, how infinitely more sad would it be to have a
voice and not want to shout." These disciples have something to shout about. They have met the risen Christ.

Malcolm Muggeridge, whom I mentioned at the outset,
was an agnostic most of his life; in his later years he was
asked to do a BBC documentary on the life of Christ. So,
with a camera crew he went to Israel. He confesses that no
place was quite as vivid to him as the road to Emmaus.
Here are his words: "Walking along with a friend I found
myself living unforgettably through the experiences of the
two travelers who took the same road shortly after the crucifixion, as described in the New Testament. So much so

that henceforth I have never doubted that whoever the wayfarers, there is always, as on that other occasion on the road to Emmaus, a third presence ready to emerge from the shadows and fall in step along the dusty stony way."

How true! That presence of Christ comes to us in the person of a friend or a wife or a husband. Sometimes we meet him in the reading of a book, in the sounds of silence, or in the great music of the church. But he comes. He comes unexpectedly and drives the gloom from our lives and transforms low Sunday into a mountaintop experience. May that be your experience!

10. Ascension

He Ascended into Heaven

So when they had come together, they asked him, "Lord, is this the time when you will restore the kingdom to Israel?" He replied, "It is not for you to know the times or periods that the Father has set by his own authority. But you will receive power when the Holy Spirit has come upon you; and you will be my witnesses in Jerusalem, in all Judea and Samaria, and to the ends of the earth." When he had said this, as they were watching, he was lifted up, and a cloud took him out of their sight. While he was going and they were gazing up toward heaven, suddenly two men in white robes stood by them. They said, "Men of Galilee, why do you stand looking up toward heaven? This Jesus, who has been taken up from you into heaven, will come in the same way as you saw him go into heaven." (Acts 1:6-11)

Last Thursday was Ascension Day. For many centuries the four major festivals of the Christian church were Christmas, Easter, Ascension, and Pentecost. Christmas and Easter are duly observed in our churches, for even our secular society acknowledges these two seasons of the year. Yet we may question the manner in which they are celebrated.

Pentecost, which we will remember to celebrate next

Sunday, gets a fair amount of attention within our churches, partly because it always falls on a Sunday. But Ascension Day has fallen into neglect. The major reason is that it always comes on a Thursday which is not a public holiday. Since most of our calendars do not even mark it as Ascension Day, we can easily overlook this great event altogether.

When I was still in public school, our church, in a rural community, observed Ascension Day rather carefully. On one occasion several of us boys decided we would leave school and go to church instead. It was not our piety that led to this decision but the chance to skip out of school. The next day we were severely reprimanded by the principal, who assured us that he had nothing against going to church. But when school was called, we were to be in our places.

I have no intention of crusading for a public holiday at Ascensiontide, but we had better make sure that we do not forget the great historic event of Christ's exaltation. It belongs to those great once-for-all happenings which form the bedrock on which the Christian faith is built.

For the report on the ascension, we must turn to the book of Acts, Luke's second volume. Yet let us also note allusions to Christ's ascension in the Gospels. Repeatedly Jesus spoke of ascending to the Father. "What if you were to see the Son of Man ascending to where he was before?" he asks his disciples (John 6:62). And to Mary Magdalene the risen Christ said, "Do not hold on to me, because I have not yet ascended to the Father" (John 20:17).

There is a brief reference to the ascension in Mark's longer ending. Some Bibles have this in the footnotes because it is not found in many of the earlier manuscripts. Matthew makes no reference to the ascension at all. Luke's Gospel, however, closes with a clear statement on the ascension, although it is but an endnote to the Gospel. Luke must have planned to write a second volume, and he makes the ascension the connecting link between his Gospel and the Acts of the Apostles.

Let us then turn to the story of Christ's ascension as it is recorded in Acts 1:6-11, and listen to its message. The Apostles' Creed, confessed by the church from the fourth century on, says, "He ascended into heaven." And that shall be our topic for this morning's message: Christ ascended into heaven. First, enter this event with me.

The Historical Event

The Account of the Event

In the forty days following his glorious resurrection from the dead, our Lord appears to his disciples again and again. He enlarges their understanding of the message which he has proclaimed throughout his ministry: The coming of the kingdom of God (Acts 1:3). In the light of the cross and the resurrection, that message takes on new meaning. Unfortunately, the disciples of Jesus are still not free from nationalistic and political understandings of this kingdom. They continue to ask, *Lord, is this the time when you will restore the kingdom to Israel?* (Acts 1:6).

Our Lord does not really entertain their question. He has made it abundantly clear that his kingdom is not from this world (John 19:36). So in response he reminds his followers, instead, of their mission during the interim between Christ's ascension and his return in glory. He repeats the great commission which he had given earlier and even suggests the ground plan of this mission: from Jerusalem to Judea, Samaria, and to the ends of the earth (Acts 1:8). This is in keeping with the hopes of the prophets that from Jerusalem, salvation would come for the world.

This assignment is far beyond the capabilities of Christ's followers, and thus our Lord assures them that they will receive the power to carry out this mission to the world.

The disciples are asked to remain in Jerusalem until they are baptized with the Holy Spirit, until they are empowered by the Spirit (Acts 1:5, 8).

Having said that, Jesus takes his disciples to the Mount of Olives, outside Jerusalem, and there he is taken away from them. *He was lifted up, and a cloud took him out of their sight* (Acts 1:9). They have seen him vanish from before their eyes on other occasions, but now he vanishes not to appear again until that day when this age comes to an end and the Son of Man appears in clouds of glory.

The cloud enveloped Christ at his transfiguration; in a cloud he vanishes into the heavens; and in the clouds he will come again to gather all the saints and bring them to the Father's house. Already in Old Testament times, the cloud was a symbol of divine hiddenness and of revelation, mystery, and majesty.

The disciples continue to gaze into the sky, hoping, no doubt, that the cloud will dissolve and that they will see Jesus again. In the past several weeks, the risen Christ has revealed himself repeatedly and then vanished. However, two heavenly messengers appear and explain to the disciples that their Lord has been taken up into heaven and that he will not return until the end of the age.

That's about as brief an account of the ascension as one could possibly give. Just a thumbnail sketch. Two verses, to be exact. Verses 9 and 10 report that Jesus goes into heaven, and verse 11 records the words of the angelic messengers. In just a few bold strokes with his pen, Luke reports one of the most important events of all times.

The Believability of the Event

There are Bible readers who have no difficulty accepting the historicity of Christ's incarnation, his marvelous life, and his cruel death. But when they come to the resurrection and the ascension, they stop short. Their minds have been shaped so deeply by the modern scientific world-view that they shrink back at teachings that obviously take us out of our depths. Clearly, when we speak of the resurrection and the ascension, we are in the realm of the miraculous, the mysterious, the majestic.

Frank Morrison was a young British lawyer strongly influenced by the rationalism of the day and by the demand for evidence by his profession. He writes that he had no trouble reciting the Apostles' Creed until he came to the articles, "He rose on the third day," followed by the confession, "He ascended into heaven." He used to stop dead at this point in the Anglican Service, in which the Creed is regularly confessed. He simply refused to utter such words. So he set himself the task of stripping the Christian faith of such primitive beliefs, as he thought them to be. By the grace of God, in the process of his research, God invaded his life, and he became a humble child of God. Then he realized that these unique events are the very foundation stones of the Christian faith.

We know that these overwhelming acts of God in Christ cannot be investigated by the tools of scientific research, but they can be grasped by the hands of faith. When embraced with heart and soul, they make a lot of sense. Indeed, if one removes one of these foundation stones of the gospel, the whole building collapses. Christ's perfect life and his atoning death are made of no effect.

For the early Evangelists, the ascension of Christ was as much a historical event as was his death on the cross. They were witnesses of this event. Here they stand on the Mount of Olives and see the Christ taken away before their eyes. In his Gospel Luke adds an interesting touch to his brief note on the ascension: They "returned to Jerusalem with great joy" (Luke 24:52).

The Joy of the Event

We have all had to say good-bye to someone we loved dearly, and it was painful to us. We have walked up and down the platform of a railway station, wishing the train would go, so that the agony of parting would come to an end. Today most of the sad good-byes are said in airports. What lover ever sang praises when the loved one departed? What heart was ever blithe in the moment of farewell? How astonishing, then, to read at the end of Luke's Gospel, "And they worshiped him, and returned to Jerusalem with great joy; and they were continually in the temple blessing God" (Luke 24:52-53).

There were those last never-to-be-forgotten weeks together with Jesus, those infinitely precious moments of conversation, and then the final walk to the Mount of Olives along the familiar road they often traveled in the past. Then suddenly they are alone. They ought to be desolate and brokenhearted, bereaved and forlorn. But no, they rejoice!

Several weeks earlier Jesus told them that he would be going away, and that announcement sent shivers down their back. "It is expedient . . . that I go away," said Jesus (John 16:7, KJV). Expedient? What advantage is there in being left orphans? What on earth did the Master mean? Well, now they know. This farewell is not the end of hope; it is its glorious verification. This is God's final Yes to everything Jesus has said and done. And once this truth sinks in, they see deeper and profounder meanings in the ascension. To these we turn next.

Theological Interpretation of the Ascension

Completing Christ's Work of Redemption

Ascension completed what was begun at the incarnation. In 1 Timothy 3:16 we have a stanza from an early Christian hymn. It has six lines. The writer begins with

Christ's incarnation: "He was revealed in flesh," and in the last line confesses, "taken up in glory."

What was begun when Christ was born, was completed when he was exalted on high. "He ascended," writes Paul to the Ephesians; "what does it mean but that he had also descended into the lower parts of the earth" (Eph. 4:9). The descent he has in mind is the incarnation, embracing his entire earthly existence. And the ascension is the final act of this drama of redemption. When Luke says, "He . . . was carried up into heaven," he means that God took him back to glory (Luke 24:51). That was God's way of putting his stamp of approval on the work of his Son.

Christ's ascension, however, not only completes what was begun at the incarnation. It also puts the capstone on the work of redemption accomplished on Calvary. The writer to the Hebrews begins his great epistle with this affirmation: "When he had made purification for sins, he sat down at the right hand of the Majesty on high" (Heb. 1:3). And again, "When Christ had offered for all time a single sacrifice for sins, 'he sat down at the right hand of God' " (Heb. 10:12).

This writer declares that Jesus, "for the sake of the joy that was set before him endured the cross, disregarding its shame, and has taken his seat at the right hand of the throne of God" (Heb. 12:2). His exaltation turned the tragedy of Golgotha into a door of hope for all who believe.

More frequently, however, the ascension is connected with Christ's resurrection. Some even think we ought not to distinguish too sharply between the two, for the ascension is but the second stage of the exaltation, with the resurrection being the first stage. In Ephesians 1:20 Paul speaks of the overwhelming power which God displayed in Christ "when he raised him from the dead and seated him at his right hand in the heavenly places." And that is only one of many passages in which the resurrection and the ascension are tied together.

Moreover, the ascension of Christ paved the way for the coming of his Spirit. "This Jesus God raised up, and of that all of us are witnesses," said Peter in his Pentecost sermon. But then he continued, "Being therefore exalted at the right hand of God, and having received from the Father the promise of the Holy Spirit, he has poured out this that you both see and hear" (Acts 2:32-33). Next Sunday we shall hear more about the coming of the Spirit as we celebrate Pentecost.

The ascension, as we have seen, is an integral part of the whole Christ event. It completes the earthly career of our Lord; it is God's great Yes to Christ's work on earth.

Proclaiming Christ's Victory over All Evil Powers

The writer to the Hebrews explains that God said to Jesus—not to angels, but to Jesus, "Sit at my right hand until I make your enemies a footstool for your feet" (Heb. 1:13, from Ps. 110:1). That's an oriental metaphor for the complete subjection of enemies; the conqueror steps on them.

That Christ is the Conqueror is underscored particularly in the book of Revelation. "I myself conquered," says the risen Christ to the churches of Asia, "and sat down with my Father on his throne" (Rev. 3:21). His enthronement was the sign that he had overcome all evil powers. Redemption is described by a great many figures of speech in the New Testament. One of these is what is called the Christus-victor motif. This victor motif is found also in the story of Israel's deliverance from Pharaoh's clutches. Israel's God triumphed over the Egyptians and their gods and delivered God's people out of bondage.

Similarly, Christ's life was a struggle with evil powers. He describes himself as the Stronger One who enters into the strong man's house, the devil's, and robs him of his goods—the people whom he held in bondage (Mark 3:27;

Luke 8:21-22). As Jesus faced the cross, he assured his disciples that now the prince of this world would be cast out. And when Christ rose triumphantly from the grave and ascended into heaven, "he disarmed the rulers and authorities and made a public example of them, triumphing over them" (Col. 2:15).

Christ, writes Peter, "has gone into heaven and is at the right hand of God, with angels, authorities, and powers made subject to him" (1 Pet. 3:22). And to the Ephesians, Paul wrote, that when Christ ascended on high, "he took captives into captivity" (Eph. 4:8, REB; cf. 1:21; Ps. 68:18).

They nailed Jesus to the tree, but by that very act he brought the world to his feet. They gave him a cross, not realizing that he would make it a throne. They flung him outside the gates of Jerusalem to die, not knowing that in that very moment the gates of the universe were opened to receive the king of glory. They thought they had him pinned to the wall, helpless and defeated, but he led all his enemies in a train of triumph.

We know that evil powers are still oppressing God's people, but it's only a matter of time. The godlessness, the barbarism, the deceit, the corruption that is so prevalent in our society today—all these will one day come to an end, and the kingdoms of this world will in truth belong to the crucified Galilean.

Psalm 8 called for all things to be in subjection to human beings, *the son of man,* which in the New Testament is a title of the Christ. The writer of Hebrews admits that "we do not yet see everything in subjection . . . but we do see Jesus, who for a little while was made lower than the angels, now crowned with glory and honor because of the suffering of death"; God will finish putting all things under his feet (Heb. 2:6-9). Because he triumphed when he ascended into heaven, he today is the exalted Lord over all, even those who do not yet recognize him.

Declaring That Jesus Is Lord of All

To the Philippians, Paul writes that after Christ's abject humiliation and shameful death on the cross, "God also highly exalted him and gave him the name that is above every name, so that at the name of Jesus every knee should bend . . . and every tongue should confess that Jesus Christ is Lord, to the glory of God the Father" (Phil. 2:9-11).

And to the Ephesians he writes that God seated Christ "at his right hand in the heavenly places, far above all rule and authority and power and dominion, and above every name that is named, not only in this age but also in the age to come. And he has put all things under his feet and has made him the head over all things for the church" (Eph. 1:20-22).

Among Gentile Christians, as far as we know, the earliest confession of faith was simply, "Jesus is Lord." People are saved by confessing that Jesus is Lord (Rom. 10:9-10). He is Lord not only of the entire universe; he is Lord also of the church; and he is Lord of our individual lives.

Dietrich Bonhoeffer wrote from prison: "Today is Ascension Day and a great joy for all who can believe that Christ rules the world and our lives." Bonhoeffer wrote that line when the forces of evil appeared to rule the world, evil powers that in the end put him to death.

About the middle of the second century, the aged Polycarp of Smyrna was taken into the arena of the city, condemned because of his faith. He looked up to heaven and said, "Lord God, the Ruler of all . . . I bless you, and glorify you above all things through Jesus Christ . . . through whom is glory to you with him and the Holy Spirit now and for ages to come. Amen." And then they lit the fire that consumed him.

"He is Lord. He is risen from the dead and he is Lord. Every knee shall bow, every tongue confess, that Jesus Christ is Lord."

Setting the Stage for Christ's Return at the End of the Age

The Apostles' Creed confesses this about Jesus Christ: "He ascended into heaven, and sitteth on the right hand of God the Father Almighty; from thence he shall come to judge the quick and the dead." As the apostles gazed into heaven, the heavenly messengers explained that the Jesus whom they had seen ascending was the Jesus who would come at the end of the age.

Ascension Day is a strong reminder for us that the day is coming when every eye shall see him. Those who pierced him and rejected him will wail in bitter remorse (Rev. 1:7).

These then are some of the theological interpretations which the new Testament writers have given us. Let me conclude by asking what might be some of the practical implications of the ascension of Jesus into glory.

Practical Implications of the Ascension

Christ Interceding for Us

Christ is the great high priest who is now "exalted above the heavens," says the writer to the Hebrews (7:25-26). "We have such a high priest, one who is seated at the right hand of the throne of the Majesty in the heavens" (Heb. 8:1).

Paul also connects the exaltation of Christ with his intercessory activity. "Who will bring any charge against God's elect? It is God who justifies. Who is to condemn? It is Christ Jesus, who died, yes, who was raised, who is at the right hand of God, who indeed intercedes for us" (Rom. 8:33-34).

Satan is constantly accusing us. One of his names is "the accuser of our comrades." He is said to accuse the children of God night and day (Rev. 12:10). Our own sins often accuse us too; our consciences condemn us. But our Lord who is seated at the right hand of God intercedes for us. God does not want us to sin, but if we do sin, says the apostle John, "we have an advocate with the Father, Jesus Christ the righteous," who speaks in our defense (1 John 2:1). The Greek word for *advocate* is *paraklētos* and means, literally, *one who is called alongside to help.* In the legal sense it means *a person who intercedes on our behalf.*

Charles Wesley sings so beautifully: "He ever lives above, For me to intercede, His all redeeming love, His precious blood to plead; His blood atoned for all our race, and sprinkles now the throne of grace."

Christ Present with Us Today

In his farewell discourses, our Lord assured his disciples that he would not leave them orphans even if he went away (John 14:18). Indeed, he said it was to their advantage that he go away, for if he did not go away, the Advocate or Counselor would not come to help them (John 16:7). If Jesus had remained physically present in Judea or Galilee, then people in the rest of the world would be at a great disadvantage. But he has ascended, writes Paul, "so that he might fill all things" (Eph. 4:10); he pervades the universe. By his Spirit, Christ is everywhere.

And so we can be sure that Christ is with us in our assembly, for he promised that where two or three are gathered in his name, he would be among them (Matt. 18:20). He is also with us in our loneliness. Samuel Rutherford languished in a Scottish prison cell for his faith. Some may attribute his lines to fever and delirium, but I think they came from faith: "Jesus Christ came into my cell last night, and every stone flashed like a ruby."

Christ is with the laborer in the daily tasks. He is with us in the tragedies of life, in our sorrows and disappointments. He is with us as we carry out the great commission. The Gospel of Matthew closes with the command to go into all the world and make disciples of all nations. Following this command comes the word of assurance: "And remember, I am with you always, to the end of the age" (Matt. 28:18-20).

When Paul came to the wicked city of Corinth, he confessed that he was full of fear and trembling. But one night the Lord stood by him and said, "[Paul], do not be afraid, but speak and do not be silent; for I am with you" (Acts 18:9-10).

In the last book of the Bible, John has a vision of the exalted Christ. He sees him in his glory and majesty. But there is another dimension to the vision. The exalted Christ walks among the churches. In the midst of their temptations, their weaknesses, their sufferings, their labors, their triumphs. "Days there may be of darkness and distress, when sin has power to tempt and care to press. Yet in the darkest day I will not fear, for mid the shadows thou wilt still be near."

Christ Receiving Us When We Die

We have a vivid illustration of this in Acts 7, where Stephen, Christ's faithful servant, is stoned to death. His sermon had angered his Jewish opponents so much that they were ready to tear him to pieces. But Stephen, full of the Holy Spirit, "gazed into heaven and saw the glory of God and Jesus standing at the right hand of God" (Acts 7:55). Normally the formula is "*seated* at the right hand of God," but here Jesus stands! He is standing to welcome Stephen home to heaven; standing to cheer him on; standing like the angels of God's presence, ready to serve the saints; standing as a witness to defend his faithful martyr's witness and to vindicate him. Jesus had promised that those who confessed him before men would be vindicated before God.

Of the faithful witnesses in the book of Revelation who are killed by the enemies of the gospel, we read, "Then they heard a loud voice from heaven saying to them,

'Come up here!' And they went up to heaven in a cloud while their enemies watched them" (Rev. 14:13). No wonder John adds, "Blessed are the dead who from now on die in the Lord" (Rev. 11:12).

To be with Christ is so wonderful that Paul didn't always know which to choose: to stay here on earth and labor for Christ; or "to depart and be with Christ, for that is far better" (Phil. 1:23). Should the Lord tarry, all of us will be called upon, sooner or later, to walk through the valley of the shadow of death. That could be the loneliest hour of our existence. Our mother and father, our wife or husband, our friends cannot go with us, even though they may be present to comfort us. We have to die alone. Really? No, the risen and exalted Lord will take us by the hand and lead us to glory, and we are surrounded by the saints of all ages (Heb. 12:1; Rev. 22:1-5).

Before he died, Jesus prayed, "Father, I desire that those also, whom you have given me, may be with me where I am, to see my glory, which you have given me because you loved me" (John. 17:24). That prayer of Jesus has been answered thousands of times when in the hour of their death, Christ welcomed his children home to glory.

"At present," writes C. S. Lewis, "we are on the outside of the world, the wrong side of the door. . . . But all the leaves of the New Testament are rustling with the rumor that it will not always be so. Some day, God willing, we shall go in."

And that happens because Christ ascended into heaven.

11. Pentecost

Born of the Spirit

Now there was a Pharisee named Nicodemus, a leader of the Jews. He came to Jesus by night and said to him, "Rabbi, we know that you are a teacher who has come from God; for no one can do these signs that you do apart from the presence of God." Jesus answered him, "Very truly, I tell you, no one can see the kingdom of God without being born from above." Nicodemus said to him, "How can anyone be born after having grown old? Can one enter a second time into the mother's womb and be born?" Jesus answered, "Very truly, I tell you, no one can enter the kingdom of God without being born of water and Spirit. What is born of the flesh is flesh, and what is born of the Spirit is spirit. Do not be astonished that I said to you, 'You must be born from above.' The wind blows where it chooses, and you hear the sound of it, but you do not know where it comes from or where it goes. So it is with everyone who is born of the Spirit." (John 3:1-8)

When the Spirit of God began to move deeply in the life of John Bunyan, he tried to reform himself outwardly in life and manners. Although his heart was as wicked as ever, he did impress his neighbors with the change. Indeed, he was inclined to think that he pleased God as much as anyone else in seventeenth-century England.

But the Spirit of God opened his blinded eyes to the hardness of what he later called his "unweldable" heart. Smitten in conscience, he came upon three or four women one day, sitting at the door of a house on one of the streets of Bedford. Bunyan recalls: "I drew near to them, for I was now a brisk talker about religion. I heard, but I understood not; for they were far above me, out of my reach; for their talk was about a new birth, the work of God in their hearts." And that brings us to the theme of the passage we have just read.

Nicodemus is no less surprised than Bunyan when Jesus teaches him that he has to be *born again* (John 3:3, KJV). How utterly shattered his self-esteem! Jesus tells him, a learned rabbi, that unless he is born anew, he can not enter the kingdom of God. That would be like directing a bishop of a prestigious church to go to the rescue mission downtown and get saved.

Here is a man of high position, a ruler of the Jews, a member of the Sanhedrin, the high court of Israel. Moreover, he represents the religion of Judaism at its best, for he is a Pharisee. No doubt he is longing for the kingdom to come. He may want to talk to Jesus about that very subject.

He comes to Jesus at night. Perhaps he is afraid to let his fellow-Pharisees know the message of Jesus has somehow grabbed him. Also, according to some rabbinic teachers, the night is a good time to study the Torah; workers, freed from their other tasks, have some time. Yet Nicodemus may have come at night so he could have Jesus all to himself without being interrupted by others. The writer of John's Gospel has a tendency to use words with more than one level of meaning, and so it is probable that the word *night* is meant to suggest also the spiritual darkness in which Nicodemus lives in spite of keeping his religious scruples.

Nicodemus opens the conversation with some kind

words about Jesus. He acknowledges him as a teacher come from God. Some of his contemporaries accuse Jesus of demon possession, but Nicodemus has heard an authentic prophetic note in the sayings of Jesus. The signs which he has done have convinced Nicodemus that Jesus is an accredited prophet.

Jesus, however, whose spiritual eyes are like a flame of fire (Rev. 1:14), cuts through all pleasantries and lays his finger on the deepest need of Nicodemus's heart. Nicodemus, he said, you must be *born from above.* And how? By water and Spirit, Jesus says (3:5). And that shall be the theme of this morning's meditation: Born of the Spirit.

The Fact of the New Birth (John 3:3-5)

The new birth is peculiarly a Johannine concept, although other New Testament writers also speak of being born anew.[1] That doesn't mean, however, that the notion of a new birth was not prior to New Testament times. Gentiles who became members of the Jewish synagogue through circumcision and baptism were described as newborn children, and some Jewish rabbis raised the silly question as to whether a born-again Gentile man could not legitimately marry his own sister, since he had become a new person. Outside of Judaism, the concept of being born again was found in the mystery religions. Those who were initiated into these mysteries by various rites and ceremonies were said to be reborn. Of course, when Jesus used the expression *born again*, he meant something quite different (John 3:3, KJV).

The Old Testament prophets anticipated the day when God would take away the stony heart and give people a heart of flesh. But Nicodemus, for all his theological learning, thinks the whole idea of a new birth is slightly ridiculous. To enter a second time into one's mother's womb and be born again is utterly absurd, he objects. And, if understood in that baldly literal sense, Nicodemus was certainly right.

However, Jesus used the term *born again* as a figure of speech for making a new beginning, a fresh start in life. To be born again also means to be *born from above*—the Greek word *anōthen* has both meanings. Likely Jesus emphasizes *born from above*, and Nicodemus stumbles into taking it only in the literal sense: *born again*. To be born from above is also to be born again, but translators usually give us only one meaning of the word (see NRSV note).

Jesus then goes on to explain that unless a person is born from above, born again, he cannot see the kingdom of God. *To see* means *to experience*, and is more or less the same as *entering into the kingdom of God*. Jesus brings God's kingdom; with his coming God's reign is being established over the hearts and lives of men and women. His kingdom is a present reality. One can see it with the eyes of faith; one may enter it by confessing Christ as Lord.

There is, however, a future dimension to this kingdom which we cannot see as yet. When this age comes to an end, when Christ returns, then the eternal kingdom in all its glory shall break in. For that kingdom, coming and to come, Jesus taught us to pray: "Thy kingdom come!"

The Necessity of the New Birth (John 3:6-7)

In answer to Nicodemus's protest, Jesus explains, *What is born of the flesh is flesh, and what is born of the Spirit is spirit. Do not be astonished that I said to you, "You must be born from above."* The need for the new birth lies in the fact that we are all born of the flesh only. We need another birth—a birth by the Spirit.

Jesus is not saying, as the Gnostics did, that physical birth is evil. The word *flesh* is used here somewhat like the word *body*, and not (as so often in Paul) for that evil power that has invaded our lives. But to be born of human parentage does not automatically guarantee us entrance into the kingdom of God. To enter God's kingdom, we have to be born of the Spirit.

Nicodemus knows it is absurd to think of entering a second time into the mother's womb, to be born a second time. Jesus reminds him of the obvious: that would mean to be born of the flesh again. Another physical birth, if such a thing were possible, would not bring us any closer to the kingdom. Such a birth is on the horizontal level, we might say; the new birth occurs vertically, *from above.*

People experience this new birth in different ways. For some it means a radical upheaval that turns their life upside down. Others experience the new birth more quietly. Children who grow up in Christian homes often accept Christian values along the way, and when they give their lives to Christ, the change is not always so radical. However, Christian parentage, a Christian home, Christian values and practices—these are quite insufficient for entrance into the kingdom. That which is born of the flesh is flesh. We need a second birth, a birth by the Spirit of God. The new birth is a miracle of divine grace. And so we need to ponder the means of the new birth.

The Means of the New Birth (John 3:5)

How can anyone be born after having grown old? asks Nicodemus. We might add, "How can a person be born again when still young?"

Does Nicodemus really not understand what Jesus means when he speaks of a new birth? Or, is he so fascinated with Jesus' answer that he pretends he has not grasped what Jesus said and wants to draw him out a bit more? There are many older men and women who would love to start all over again. Some seek to rejuvenate themselves by natural and sometimes by not-so-natural means. What a thrilling prospect: to begin life over again!

But that's not what Jesus means. Is it not interesting that Jesus, who healed the sick and cleansed the lepers and even raised the dead, never once made an old person young?

How can a person be born again? Nicodemus questions. Jesus answers, *By water and Spirit.* Just as the Spirit of God exercised his creative powers at the dawn of the first creation (Gen. 1:2), so the Spirit of God can create a new life. But why water?

One answer is that water stands for human birth. Some rabbis spoke of natural birth as a birth by water. By adding *Spirit,* Jesus would then be saying, You have to have an additional birth. Being born of water is physical birth; being born by the Spirit is spiritual birth.

Others hold that water is a reference to baptism, and that may well be the way the Evangelist and his Christian readers took it (cf. John 1:33; 3:22, 26). In the early church baptism by water and the gift of the Spirit always go together, as the baptism stories of the book of Acts clearly show (Acts 2:38; cf. Tit. 3:5).

There is another way of understanding Jesus' words to Nicodemus. Since he is speaking to a teacher of Israel, who presumably knows the Hebrew Scriptures, he may well have in mind the words of God in Ezekiel: "I will sprinkle clean water upon you, and you shall be clean. . . . A new heart I will give you, and a new spirit I will put within you"(Ezek. 36:25-27).

The new birth, then, is possible only by an inner cleansing, signified by water, and by the recreative work of God's Spirit. Paul puts these two aspects of the new birth next to each other in Titus 3:5: "[God] saved us, not because of any works of righteousness that we had done, but according to his mercy, through the water of rebirth and renewal by the Holy Spirit."

It is by the Spirit of God that our consciences are awakened so that we see the need for a new life. It is by the Spirit of God that we are convicted of our sinfulness. The Spirit opens our hearts so that we give the message of the gospel a hearing. The Spirit also makes it possible for us to respond to the gospel in faith and obedience and to embrace God's offer of eternal life.

The Spirit of God, however, is not under our control. The Spirit works sovereignly and mysteriously.

The Mystery of the New Birth (John 3:8)

The wind blows where it chooses, and you hear the sound of it, but you do not know where it comes from or where it goes. So it is with everyone who is born of the Spirit.

To anyone brought up in the Jewish tradition, it was natural, almost inevitable, to compare the Spirit of God with the wind. In the Hebrew tongue the same word was used for both. The word *ruakh* can mean *breath, wind,* and *spirit. Ruakh* also designates God's Spirit—that supernatural power that sweeps across the ages, that bursts into history, that takes possession of people's lives and transforms them.

In Greek we have a similar situation. The word *pneuma* means both *wind* and *spirit.* I discovered that when fanning mills for cleaning seed grain were first introduced into Scotland, some pious folk objected to them because Jesus said the wind blows where it wills; but now people were making it blow where it did not will. That's hardly what Jesus had in mind.

Equally perverse is the charge of some worldly-wise weatherman who says that Jesus is wrong at this point. The wind does not blow where it wills; it blows according to fixed laws. But the example from nature which Jesus uses here makes perfectly good sense.

For all we know, a gust of wind may be sweeping

through the narrow streets of Jerusalem at that very moment when Jesus and Nicodemus are closeted together. Jesus says, "Nicodemus, you hear the wind, don't you? But you can't explain where it comes from nor where it goes. Well, the new birth is just as mysterious."

We are constantly amazed at the powerful working of God's Spirit, the wind of God. At times it blows with a still small voice. At other times it sweeps through a church, a school, a community like a tornado. There have been times in the history of the church when its spiritual life seemed almost extinct. But then in sovereign freedom, the wind of the Spirit swept into a valley of dry bones, and we had a great spiritual awakening.

It blows into lives that are conscious of failures, emptiness, dissatisfaction, and sin. It also blows into lives that are content, complacent, smug, and satiated. It transforms people; makes them alive for God and the things that are eternal.

George Whitefield, the great evangelist, grew up in a tavern in England, where he kept company with godless youths. Then came the sudden arrest. God's Spirit moved into his life. He tried to reform his ways, but to no avail. He went off to Oxford, and there Charles Wesley gave him a book to read. Later he wrote: "When I read this, a ray of divine light instantaneously darted in upon my soul; and from that moment . . . did I know that I must become a new creature."

He remembered all his life the very place where the words of Jesus about the new birth became for him God's call into the kingdom, and he returned to that place again and again to commemorate the great event. The new birth became a central theme in his preaching on both sides of the Atlantic. "Why, Mr. Whitefield," inquired a friend one day, "why do you so often preach on the new birth?" "Because," replied Whitefield, "ye must be born again."

Return with me for a moment to the streets of Bedford and to John Bunyan. He listened to those womenfolk on the doorstep talk about the new birth. And he writes: "They spoke as if joy made them speak; they spoke with such pleasantness of scriptural language and with such appearance of grace in all they said, that they were to me as if they had found a new world, and my heart began to shake as mistrusting my condition; for I saw in all my thoughts about religion and salvation, the new birth had never entered my mind."

He left them there on the doorstep, convinced that he needed to be born again, but he returned several times to talk with them. And then God gave him great softness and tenderness of heart. He went to church, where he heard the gospel and, as he puts it, "was so taken up with the love and mercy of God that I could hardly contain myself till I got home. I thought I could have spoken of God's love and mercy even to the crows that sat on the plowed land." He had experienced the new birth.

Here is Nicodemus. He comes to Jesus by night. He can not dream what this encounter with Jesus will lead to. The wind of the Spirit begins to blow into his life. That wind will move him to be a secret believer and speak in defense of Jesus before the Sanhedrin (John 7:50-51; 12:42). It will carry him one day to Pontius Pilate's council chamber to claim the body of Jesus—one of the boldest actions in the passion story—and beyond that to the world-shattering event of the resurrection (John 19:38-42).

In some ways it's a daunting, even frightening thought to contemplate what the Spirit of God can do with our lives. Youths may have careers mapped out, and then the Spirit of God invades their lives and takes them in an entirely different direction. There are Christian young people who don't know what to do with their lives. Perhaps they feel that they can't do much anyway; they feel so inferior, so inadequate. And then God's Spirit begins to work in their lives and harness their energies. The Spirit gives their lives a center and transforms them into useful instruments in the kingdom of God. It's happening all the time.

Benjamin Jowett of England was preparing a sermon on the wind of the Spirit, on the new birth. He decided to walk to the nearby beach where the breakers of the North Sea were coming in. There he saw a sailor. Ah, he thought, I'll ask him if he understands the mystery of the wind. He approached him and asked him to explain the wind for him. Just at that moment a sailboat appeared, plowing through the waters. The sailor replied, "Sir, I can't explain the wind, but I tell you what I can do: I can hoist a sail."

We can't explain the mysterious work of God in people's lives, but perhaps we can hoist a sail; perhaps we can get in the path of the wind and so begin to experience something of its power.

Notes

Preface
1. James S. Stewart, *Heralds of God,* 110-111.

Chapter 1: Advent
1. C. S. Lewis, *Mere Christianity* (New York: Macmillan, 1964).
2. From the hymn "O How Shall I Receive Thee."

Chapter 3: Christmas
1. Cf. "Invictus," by W. E. Henley.

Chapter 4: New Year
1. The birth of Jesus occurred some time before early 4 B.C., when Herod the Great died: Matt. 2:19.
2. Jesus began his ministry around the fifteenth year of the reign of the emperor Tiberius (Luke 3:1).
3. There are similar sounds and perhaps similar meaning in the Aramaic word for *Nazareth* and the Hebrew for *branch:* Isa. 11:1 (the Davidic Messiah); Matt. 2:23.
4. The Shema is Israel's confession of faith from Deut. 6:4: "Hear [Hebrew: *shema*], O Israel! The Lord is our God, the Lord alone" (see NRSV note).
5. Stephen Travis, *I Believe in the Second Coming of Jesus* (Grand Rapids: Eerdmans, 1982), 57.

Chapter 5: Lent
1. James I. Packer, *God's Words* (Downers Grove, Ill.: Inter-Varsity Press, 1982), 71.
2. C. S. Lewis, *Mere Christianity* (New York: Macmillan, 1964).
3. Richard Holloway, *A New Heaven,* 36.

4. P. T. Forsyth, *The Work of Christ* (London: Collins, 1965), 42ff.

Chapter 7: Good Friday
1. Richard B. Gardner, *Matthew* (Scottdale, Pa.: Herald Press, 1991), 383.

Chapter 8: Easter
1. The Gospel of the Hebrews, quoted by Jerome, *On Illustrious Men* 2.
2. Josephus, *Antiquities* 20.9.1; Eusebius, *Ecclesiastical History* 1.23; 2.1; 2.23.

Chapter 9: Low Sunday
1. Quoted in A. M. Hunter, *Bible and Gospel,* 110.
2. Gospel of Thomas 77, available in editions of the New Testament Apocrypha such as W. Schneemelcher, ed., *New Testament Apocrypha,* vol. 1, rev. ed. (Louisville: Westminster John Knox, 1990).

Chapter 11: Pentecost
1. Cf. 1 John 3:9 and elsewhere: "born of God"; 1 Pet. 1:23, "born anew"; Tit. 3:5: "water of rebirth and renewal of the Holy Spirit."

The Author

David Ewert's life began in the Mennonite colony of Memrik, in the Ukraine, where his parents belonged to the Mennonite Brethren (MB) Church. After the Russian Revolution and the following famine, during which David was born in 1922, the family emigrated to Canada. They moved from place to place to find work and finally settled on a farm at Coaldale, Alberta. Ewert obtained his elementary education there and as a youth was converted to Christ and baptized in the Coaldale MB congregation.

Ewert attended Bible institutes for five years before he married Lena Hamm, from northern Alberta. They have five married children and twelve grandchildren. After marriage, David taught in Bible institutes for seven years while also continuing his education.

After David completed his B.A. at the University of British Columbia and graduated from seminary in Toronto, the Ewerts moved to Winnipeg. There he taught Bible at the MB Bible College for nineteen years. On the side he completed other graduate degrees and earned a Ph.D. in New Testament at McGill University in Montreal.

In 1972 the Ewerts moved to Harrisonburg, Virginia, where David enjoyed three years of teaching at Eastern Mennonite Seminary and ministering in area churches and at retreats. Throughout his ministry, he has combined preaching and teaching.

When the MBs of Canada and the United States decided to cooperate in a joint seminary at Fresno, California, Ewert went west to teach New Testament there for seven years. Then he was called back to Winnipeg to be president of the MB Bible College until he was sixty-five. He and his wife are members of the Elmwood MB Church in Winnipeg.

Earlier in his career, Ewert was visiting professor in theological schools in India at Yeotmal, in South America, in Europe, and in Canada. Upon retirement he taught for two semesters at the Nairobi Graduate School of Theology.

The following year Ewert taught at the Mennonite Bible School at Bienenberg, Switzerland, and preached Bible messages in Germany, Austria, France, and for two weeks in the Soviet Union. When Ewerts returned from Europe, David taught for two more years at the Fresno MB Seminary, followed by lecturing at Columbia Bible College in Clearbrook, British Columbia, where they make their home.

Ewert has published ten books and numerous book chapters and articles in encyclopedias, dictionaries, and periodicals.